"Susan Swetnam helps us be on the lookout for the tiny 'annunciations' that punctuate—and occasionally puncture—our lives. Stepping into paintings of the annunciation, from the familiar Fra Angelico fresco to Lorenzo Lotto's clearly troubled Mary, she gives us ways to explore our own reactions and emotions when we find ourselves facing a call to change course in unexpected ways. As someone on the cusp of retirement, and who works with young people as they imagine their futures, I appreciated the many lenses Swetnam offers us to see the new seeds God might be sowing."

—Michelle Francl-Donnay, author of *Prayer, Biblical Wisdom for Seeking God* and a contributor to *Give Us This Day*

"Susan Swetnam enters a labyrinth of grieving when she's widowed at fifty-four, and through her skillful writing brings the reader along every step of the way. This intensely personal experience offers hope to many who endure incalculable loss. Her stepping stones are Renaissance paintings that depict the Annunciation, the ultimate 'yes' to an unknown script. The author is brutally honest about the shock of interrupting an imagined life's trajectory and luminously clear about how Mary's path might accompany. She alerts readers to 'Gabriel surrogates' and reaches the delightful point of saying to Mary, '*Oh girlfriend, I get what you're feeling.*' After twenty years, tragedy turns to treasure and desert to garden. Lucky the reader who gets to come along for the transformation."

—Kathy Coffey, contributor to *Give Us This Day*

Everyday Annunciations

On Learning to Say Yes

Susan H. Swetnam

LITURGICAL PRESS

Collegeville, Minnesota

litpress.org

1   2   3   4   5   6   7   8   9

Library of Congress Cataloging-in-Publication Data

Names: Swetnam, Susan H., author.
Title: Everyday annunciations : on learning to say yes / Susan H. Swetnam.
Description: Collegeville, Minnesota : Liturgical Press, [2024] | Includes bibliographical references. | Summary: "In Everyday Annunciations, Susan Swetnam encourages readers to imagine how their own upheavals might function as "everyday annunciations"-invitations to partner with God in new ways. Reflecting on six Renaissance paintings depicting Mary's response to her own annunciation, Swetnam acknowledges the difficulty of regrouping when life changes radically. Everyday Annunciations draws on Mary's example, wisdom figures both historical and contemporary, Scripture, and personal narrative"— Provided by publisher.
Identifiers: LCCN 2024012809 (print) | LCCN 2024012810 (ebook) | ISBN 9798400800672 (trade paperback) | ISBN 9798400800689 (epub) | ISBN 9780814688939 (pdf)
Subjects: LCSH: Mary, Blessed Virgin, Saint—Annunciation. | Acceptance in the Bible. | Trust in God. | Christian life. | BISAC: RELIGION / Christian Living / Spiritual Growth
Classification: LCC BT615 .S93 2025 (print) | LCC BT615 (ebook) | DDC 232.91/2—dc23/eng/20240520
LC record available at https://lccn.loc.gov/2024012809
LC ebook record available at https://lccn.loc.gov/2024012810

To Ford Swetnam, Shelley McEuen-Howard, and Amy Ekeh

My best readers

Contents

Introduction   1

Chapter One
Early Annunciations: The Challenges of Youthful Vocation   17

Chapter Two
Annunciations that Change Everything:
The Fraught and Holy Path toward Acceptance   39

Chapter Three
Annunciations that Change Everything, Part Two:
Faithful Discernment as a Way Forward   61

Chapter Four
The Annunciations of Later Years:
Aging with Creative Equanimity   85

Afterword   109

Appendix: Luke's Account of the Annunciation
and *Magnificat*   115

Notes   117

For Further Reading   125

Fra Angelico (Guido di Pietro), *The Annunciation*, ca. 1438–45.

Introduction

"God's Not Going to Let You Be for Too Long"

I sat for a long time on the museum's cold stone steps one November afternoon in 2004, absorbed by the enormous fresco. Tour groups ebbed and flowed around me as they ascended to explore the riches of Renaissance art and history displayed in that space, the former monastery of the Church of San Marco in Florence, Italy. "You're still here!" someone observed with amusement—or was it concern?—on her way back down.

What had transfixed me was a famous masterpiece—the Italian painter Fra Angelico's great fifteenth-century painting of Mary's annunciation in the north dormitory hall—which triggered within me a flood of reflections about the previous three years, the bleak ones since my husband's early death from cancer. I'd come to Florence on that Thanksgiving break vaguely dreaming of encountering his spirit in this city we'd once visited so happily together, telling myself in a blur of magical thinking that he'd get to see it again through my eyes. On that vacation Ford had lingered over the paintings at San Marco, seeing something I didn't, for my senses were by then overloaded with masterpieces, and he was by far the better-schooled in art. Perhaps this time I'd see what my husband had seen, I told myself. Perhaps I'd feel his presence somewhere in this city that had spoken so deeply to him.

But up until that afternoon I'd been too consumed by my own misery to feel much of anything else. Even thousands of miles from home my blood pounded with the frantic, stress-inspired panic of extended, complicated grief; my mind blurred with a chronic inability to focus. The beautiful, interesting city proved no distraction, for I was not really there. The streets were haunted by our former passing; the museums, historic sites, gardens, and shops all blurred in a haze of loneliness and unreality. The happy energy surrounding me—which I'd hoped might buoy me up—instead felt like an affront. The world was carrying on as if nothing had happened.

As darkness fell the previous evening, I realized that I'd been standing and staring for a long time over a low railing at the cold Arno River, coursing through the midst of the city in its deep stone channel. *Wait till you get home and can sit out on the mountain slope behind the house,* I heard my mind say. *Hypothermia in an Idaho winter will hurt less, and your friends will want to know what happened.*

In retrospect I should have known there was still much to live for. Kind friends and colleagues were working hard to ensure I received morale-boosting invitations to publish and speak and serve in public humanities programming. My teaching was going very well. But those things hardly seemed to matter most of the time. After Ford's death and the loss of our life-defining community of two, I could not imagine who I might be in what felt like a bleak new world, how my existence as a childless widow at age 54 might still make sense or matter in any meaningful way.

It wasn't that I hadn't tried to cope. The bedroom floor back home was stacked with heaps of self-help grief books; a pile of cheerfully colored handouts from the bereavement group I'd faithfully attended sat on the study table. I'd been seeing a counselor weekly; I'd rebuilt my running miles and tried a new hobby (pottery—not my sport, unfortunately). Nothing had offered lasting comfort, however, and the questions still thundered: *Why us? What reason could there be for this awful change? How am I going to make any peace with this new reality? What am I supposed to do with the rest of my pathetic, lame-duck life?* I was teaching the novelist Charles Dickens in my graduate seminar that semester, and when I came upon his description of a widow as her husband's "relic," I'd nodded at the phrase's perfect alignment with how I felt.

The consolation of faith wasn't doing much for me either. Since Ford's terminal diagnosis I'd let lapse what had been quite active engagement in the local Catholic community. When the bad news came, I resigned from the ministries I'd once found so fulfilling—lector, eucharistic minister, parish council member—pleading a lack of energy and the need for time at home. Both claims were accurate. But neither should have precluded attendance at weekly Mass as his health declined and then after his death . . . and yet I largely gave that up, too, for I could not bear the pity I encountered, or the questions, which only reminded me of my loss even as I sought an hour's peace.

Truth be told, my relationship with the divine outside of church wasn't too healthy either, marked as it was by bitter confusion, feelings of anger and abandonment, and, perversely, by a scruple-fueled, dog-chasing-its-tail kind of fear that this very estrangement I felt from God demonstrated that the faith I'd once believed in so solidly must have been a charade. How many thousands of times had I so blithely, sententiously intoned "Thy will be done"? Liar.

"Give your sorrow to the Lord," well-meaning people of faith had advised. "Let go and let God." But letting go was the last thing I wanted to do. I found my fingers tightening around the past, fantasizing that my husband's death had been a bad dream, that perhaps if I just lived through one more night, I'd wake back into that beautiful reality. *Easy for you to say*, I raged internally when such advice came. *You, who get to keep your husband. Try living without the one person who truly sees you. See how easy it is to "let God" give you a bleak, lonely future.*

It was ironic, then, to say the least, that the painting which captivated my utterly noncompliant self that November afternoon in Florence depicted *the* premier, canonical archetype of surrender to a future whose contours could not be grasped: the annunciation of the Virgin Mary. "You're invited to bear in your womb the Son of God," the angel Gabriel in essence tells this young girl who'd been innocently going about her business, imagining a normal future for her time and place—a husband and children, housework and religious observances, aging in the bosom of her family. What a shock that announcement must have been, disrupting all she'd prepared for, challenging her to be another person than the one she'd imagined herself to be. Nevertheless, that maiden said "yes"—definitively—even praising the Mystery who'd just pulled the rug of normalcy out from under her (Luke 1:26-56).

But in the fresco that fascinated me that afternoon, Fra Angelico's Mary has not yet said "yes," much less come to the point of singing her *Magnificat*. Instead, she's depicted in an earlier fleeting moment of incredulity as she wonders, "How can this be?" (See appendix for Luke's account of the annunciation and *Magnificat*.)

She's hunched over, staring, appearing disoriented—visibly verging on clinical shock. Yes, I know what historians and aficionados of Annunciation art will tell me—that crossed hands, a forward-leaning posture, and a bowed head are conventional signs of Mary's humility, indicating her worthiness for this most awesome calling. Still, I invite you to look more closely at her face. It's deathly pale, and those eyes are blankly staring into space, not demurely downcast. And there are various ways of crossing one's arms. Here Mary's are tightly clasped around her core, appearing to shield, protect, and warm herself as people who've just suffered an emotional blow instinctively do.

But we can let go of the question of exactly what Fra Angelico meant, for what matters in the story I'm telling now is what I *saw* that day (and continue to see) in that rendering of the annunciation scene: tacit permission to be human, assurance that a God who understands and accepts human frailty is still lovingly present with someone who struggles with doubt, patiently waiting for her to come to terms with the destiny to which he's inviting her. *Even Mary,* I thought that afternoon, letting the reassurance flow over me. *Even Mary had at least a moment's anxious resistance when a future she couldn't imagine broke over her. Perhaps there's hope for me, too.*

On that very day my self-made impasse began to break, as a half-a-millennium-old work of art spoke truth to me about mercy and faith's evolving nature, gripping me in sudden, instinctive insight beyond the power of words. Granted, it would be five or six more years before I felt anything like stable again in my own skin—my new, God-given skin, that is. But what beautiful twists and turns, unimaginable in that dark time, have marked those days since that painting helped me take those first steps toward saying "yes" to a new understanding of what I might be called to make of my life, leading me ever-onward toward a sense of what real surrender might look like—surrender inflected with humility, yes, but also with mercy, grace, and strength—an intricate blend of divine decree and creative agency that enables a person to live as God's fully human child.

Everyday Annunciations

If you've picked up this book, I'm guessing that your life's trajectory, like mine, has been disrupted by at least one event that has challenged your comfortable expectations about how your days would play out, inviting (or dragooning) you into a future you never anticipated.

Such callings are common, after all, in every stage of human existence. I've just described a representative of the dramatic bolt-from-the-blue species—the loss of a loved one, job, or marriage; ill health or natural disaster; betrayal; revelation of a personal flaw that sullied a relationship or career. Such events are famous for causing identity crises and dark nights of the soul. Some people never really get over them, and everyone who experiences them at least bears scars.

But there are also other varieties of calling that, while quieter, more gradual, even happier, still have the capacity to upend the comfortable givens that previously anchored our days. Despite all the joy that young adults find, for instance, in settling into the occupations, marriages, parenthood, and life paths that they may believe are their foreordained destinies, circumstances will shake such youthful idealism, inviting neophytes to recast comfortable assumptions about how God might intend for them to use their gifts. Middle-aged men and women also find themselves radically disoriented when life's work or relationships evolve in unforeseen ways, when children leave home, or when their hearts begin whispering, "Is this all there is?" And the call to rethink identity and meaning continues in later years, sparked by retirement from an occupation that ordered time and defined each day's purpose, by the decline of vigor and changes in physical appearance, by loss of friends and health, by departure from a long-beloved home.

Finding a way forward when such disruptive circumstances upend a perfectly good status quo can be difficult indeed. Yet if we live long enough, some or another insistent call to evolve *will* arise, like it or not, and attempting to ignore such a summons can inspire feelings of stagnation, bitterness, and separation from ourselves, from others, even from God. A wiser course is to take a page from the Buddhists' book and grant that change is the only constant—indeed, it's the medium by which we live and move and have our being. We might be able to ignore that truth (or convince ourselves that we're able to ignore it) during those long, calm stretches in our life's path, as placid business-as-usual intervals lull us into feeling like they'll last forever. But the jostling imperative to accept transformation *will* come again, like it or not. "If you learn anything in life," said a woman for whom I used to provide hospice massages, now gone to her rest, "it's that God's never going to let you be for too long." She smiled. "You just have to trust that his pestering is for the best—for you, or at least for somebody else."

This book explores the implications of that simple, profound statement. Working from the proposition that a loving Heavenly Father has a beneficent plan for his creation, the pages that follow will frame life's disruptions as "annunciations," invitations to say "yes" to progress in ways we cannot imagine but that God has imagined for us—just like Mary's annunciation in Luke 1:26-38—even when such disruptions appear daunting, tragic, or inexplicable.

Obviously, there are vast differences between Gabriel's invitation to Mary and those extended to everyday people through such "messengers" as a new job or a job loss, a child's death, a Parkinson's diagnosis. There was only one annunciation delivered by Gabriel in history and only one Mary, perfectly created for the task through her immaculate conception, her sinless nature. The vocation of bearing God's Son is so far exalted above anything we might be summoned to accomplish that we can only bow down in awe.

Yet I'm going to insist throughout this book that the "everyday annunciations" that mark human life—those callings of vocation or unexpected, changed circumstances which push us toward new ways of being—are similar to Mary's in some ways, though in an infinitely more modest key. They challenge us, as Mary was challenged, to hold fast to our faith in the face of unforeseen, even paradigm-shattering circumstances, to open ourselves to an uncertain future. They demand that we shed the fantasy of complete control over our lives and acknowledge divine sovereignty. They call not only for us to "gestate" new aspects of ourselves and new understandings of our relationship with the Mystery, but, as Fr. Jean Pierre de Cassaude preached in his classic work on Christian surrender, to allow ourselves to be "overshadowed" by the Holy Spirit just as Mary was so Jesus can be born anew in us.[1]

And as was true in the case of Mary's acceptance, our assents require ongoing, active, creative work. While extreme expressions of "let go and let God" in contemporary popular Christian discourse might balk at the implication of human agency,[2] Mary herself, after all, was anything but inert during the months and years that followed her "yes." She honored her human desire to understand by "pondering"; she partnered with Joseph in keeping the baby Jesus safe; she stood by her Son at Golgotha. And if long-standing traditions are accurate, after Jesus' resurrection, Mary also companioned the disciples and helped spread the Good News to the wider world. Catholic teaching is unambiguous about the theological importance of Mary's free will in the work of salvation, framing her acceptance as an action that offsets Eve's disobedience. She's understood to continue in God's active service to this day, encouraging God's people through miracles, inviting and hearing their intercessions, and comforting them as they pray.

Such creative agency on the part of this "Untier of Knots," "Mediatrix of All Graces," and "Mother of Good Counsel" underlines what Scripture and accounts of holy lives also reveal: that God has never desired passive devotees. This is the God who gave all created ones the free will that Mary employed, the Heavenly Father who accepted Abraham's haggling about the math as they discussed the destruction of Sodom (Gen 18:22-33), the Jesus who said, "Take up your bed and walk" to the newly cured one (John 5:8). This is the God who time and again has inspired human initiative in such figures as the inquiring Aquinas, the feisty St. Teresa of Avila, the activist Martin Luther King, Jr., the God described in the prologue of the catechism as seeking disciples who seek to know their creator.

How could we not be "makers," after all, if we've been created in the likeness of a richly creative God, as Genesis 1:26 assures us we are, and as St. Paul explains to the Ephesians: "For we are his handiwork, created in Christ Jesus for the good works that God has prepared in advance" (2:10)? Holy creativity abounds in the stories of the saints, including St. Benedict, who in the fifth century crafted a revolutionary "Rule" for his monasteries that has promoted well-ordered communal life ever since; and St. Hildegard of Bingen, today popularly termed the "patron saint of creativity," who directed an abbey while simultaneously innovating in music, culinary arts, herbal medicine, illustration, and environmental awareness. Christian artists, musicians, and writers have understood their creative talent as a reflection of their Maker's, including author J. R. R. Tolkien of *Lord of the Rings* fame, who argued that since God's creatures "express the divine image" by using the faculties God has shared with them, artistic production in essence constitutes a form of worship.[3]

Mary herself has been celebrated by St. John Damascene as "Queen of All Creation," a phrase that resonates on multiple levels. She gave birth to Jesus, the author of our salvation. She is enthroned at her Son's side in heaven, given the power to intercede. She models for the rest of us how mere mortals might, with God's grace, actualize our generative capacities in ways beyond our wildest aspirations.

That all said, before going any further, I do want to be clear about one place where it seems to me that the "Mary's annunciation/everyday annunciation" analogy breaks down. While Mary's calling did come directly from God, this book's perspective does *not* presume that every course-shaping invitation we might experience is to be interpreted as God's direct call or will. Human flaws, confusion, orneriness, sin, accidents—and perhaps even a malevolent force—can and do, I believe, prompt events which push us in new directions. Neither do the pages that follow suggest that catastrophic events like wars, epidemics, earthquakes, etc., can be consolingly explained away as having some ultimate purpose. Such matters have challenged the best minds of human history, and regarding them, I can only refer you to those vastly wiser than I.[4]

As a consequence, this book limits itself to the more common calls to accept the disruptive circumstances that all human beings experience. Working within that familiar frame of reference, it invites you to imagine that God can use all things, even those that discomfit us, even those that appear impenetrable and disastrous to our individual comfort, to serve the divine will and our unfolding purposes in this created world. Or *can* use them, I should say, presuming that we can find a way to take the crucial step of saying "yes" as Mary did—that despite the fear of personal inadequacy, bitterness, or lost hope, we too can sooner or later bring ourselves to venture something along the lines of "Okay, God, where are you calling me now?"

This Book's Approach

Intended to be at once a reflection-starter and a guidebook, this book offers examples of many kinds of people who have experienced "everyday annunciations"—individuals from Scripture, doctors of the church, saints and other holy ones, and ordinary people aplenty. To put such stories in a broader context, it draws on commentary and research on a variety of subjects, including theology, neurology, and grief. It also includes passages that might be considered autobiography/spiritual memoir, not because I aspire to pose myself as a model of exemplary progress from despair to acceptance, but because, during the period of my own fumbling, I could have used such realistic blow-by-blow examples to reassure me that I was not the first or only person to be feeling/thinking/doing what I was, and I'm guessing you might welcome such reassurance, too. I would have been greatly cheered, too, by stories that verified God's deep wells of patience and that traced real-world examples of an all-merciful creator's willingness to "meddle" in an individual human life in ways brilliantly suited to getting that particular person's attention. I would also have welcomed any evidence that, although heavenly tough love can feel *very* tough and not like love at all when it's raining down upon us, someday we will realize that that even in those darkest days, the Father remained our loving Shepherd.

The chapters that follow discuss three sorts of everyday annunciations that commonly cause crises of both faith and identity in human life. The first chapter takes up what most people think of when they hear the word "calling": the experience of feeling pulled, especially as a young person, toward a particular sphere of service, including to a career, marriage, parenthood, religious vocation, or volunteer work. If you've encountered such a summons, whether through someone's early recognition of your talent or through personal experiences that functioned as blinking arrows, you'll surely remember the heady excitement of feeling planted where you're supposed to bloom. I certainly do . . . the rush of joy and sense of everything falling into place that I felt as a young teacher and writer, and as a thirty-something bride when my husband and I committed to a marriage that not only taught us both how to love, but also fostered our mutual potential as teachers, writers, and friends.

You'll likely also recall, however, the much less pleasant wake-up calls that almost certainly followed, as the realization dawned that your vocation was going to be much harder in its day-to-day treading, much less glamorous, than you'd expected. Other people's unexpected behaviors, your own surprising inadequacies, circumstantial differences between what you imagined this life path would be like and its actual reality, can all function as unwelcome evidence that some regrouping, at least, is in order. The everyday annunciation of vocation, it turns out, doesn't forecast a future of perfect fit, but establishes a platform on which evolution occurs.

Yet how satisfying it is, ultimately, for a young person to learn that she's capable of rising to the challenge of growth, to commit to the faith and work that can turn a vague dream into a useful, fulfilling vocation. And how helpful such baby-step practice in saying "yes" to the realities of God's world can be as it offers initial lessons in learning to respond to the cues that tell us when it's time to adjust, and in providing early practice for the more challenging course-corrections that life will later bring.

Chapter 2 takes up the subject of those wrenching events, everyday annunciations that manifest as tragedies such as a loved one's death, a dire health diagnosis or disabling injury, loss of employment, homelessness, victimization by a serious crime. When such circumstances shatter long-established routines and identities, they invite existential crises, demanding that those who experience them begin anew when they don't want to, when they doubt their capacity to do so. Questions inevitably arise: *What kind of God could let this happen to me? Who will I be without the one I love? How can I go forward now that my concept of the future has been shattered and I can't imagine any "rest of the story" that I want to embrace?*

The personal histories recorded in this chapter demonstrate that guilt, hopelessness, aridity, anger, separation from others and God, and destructive "fumbling" are common among those whose lives have been upended by such painful summons to unsought evolution. Yet despair is not a forever-sentence since, as Henri Nouwen has written, the very emptiness of loss can function to "call us to the dance" of a reimagined life, thanks to divine love.[5] Even if sufferers stay perversely, pathetically stuck at "no" for an extended period of time, according to Nouwen, a patient God who has faith in them will continue to encourage them, hoping that eventually they will open their ears, offer at least conditional acceptance, and believe that God might just have something new, something constructive, in mind.

Chapter 3 discusses the discernment that can propel such initial acceptance toward God-inflected rebirth. Cautioning readers to take their time through that process rather than attempting to recreate an "old normal" or rushing to replace uncomfortable liminality with too-neat answers, it describes the many forms that continual, prayerful conversation with God might take. Because I found Thomas Merton's and Richard Rohr's work on perceiving the false and true selves, and Nouwen's guidance on "reading the signs of daily life" especially helpful, these writers' insights are suggested as a place to begin when practicing discernment. Patiently listening for divine prompting, cultivating connection through prayer, and paying attention to indications of divine in-reaching can prove revelatory. Such practices can move the seeker to a more mature, more personal relationship with God—even if she herself doubts her capacity for such union. While not pretending that the process of turning a theoretical "yes" into active engagement is easy, or presuming that new vocations will not themselves change over time, this discussion emphasizes and encourages the transformative power of openness. Indeed, the God who said "I make all things new" (Rev 21:5) is eager to engage human beings in creative partnership, helping them reimagine their lives in a new key that accords with an intimate knowledge of their true nature and potential.

Chapter 4 explores what might follow from such acceptance as life moves toward its later "mature" phase, suggesting that those who have previously experienced the lessons everyday annunciations teach about listening and trusting are better prepared for the inevitable changes that aging brings. Though acknowledging the common challenges of old age—retirement, changes in physical appearance and declining strength, dependence on others—this section of the book describes how numerous people maturing in years and faith have found in old age a period of rich, ongoing productivity. If we have learned (or can learn) to accept divine sovereignty and to trust that God intends an "unfolding" to take place throughout our lives, then even old age can hold new blooming. . . and the habits of prayerful, trusting relationship described throughout the book can go a very long way in preserving our equanimity—our equilibrium—even as death, the most mysterious annunciation of them all, nears.

Art as a Reflective Tool

If you've already browsed through these pages, you've noticed that this book includes several works of art. Intended to encapsulate themes and engage your reflective energy in an additional, more intuitive way, the six fine art reproductions you'll find here—one for each chapter as well as for the introduction and afterword—invite you to pause and reflect on your own experience with "annunciation" and on your faith, especially your understanding of Mary.

Rest assured that you don't need training in art appreciation or theory to find in these images evocative food for thought since, as scholars in the field of art reception have explained, all humans possess the capacity to tap into self-awareness and deeper insight via the power of representational art. From babyhood, they tell us, human beings have the instinct to read others' expressions and gestures and the impulse to imitate them via "mirror neurons." Empathy grows from such awareness, along with the capacity to compare the other with oneself—even if "the other" is a shape depicted by paint, stone, or photographic processing.[6] One innovative branch of this research demonstrates by MRI imaging that we are as hardwired to empathize with painted faces as with real ones, able to put ourselves in the figures' places.[7] Further, theorists in the psychology of aesthetics have determined through experimentally rigorous study how body positions trigger viewers' understanding of represented figures' moods and relationships, and how specific features of a work of art influence similar interpretations across a large sample of viewers. Granted, not every pictured figure will be perceived as a second self, but contrast can also be enlightening— for how we interpret the attitude of a person in a painting has the potential to tell us much about how we ourselves are feeling.

The particular works of art offered for your contemplation are all Renaissance paintings based on Mary's annunciation, each inspired by the moment ("freeze-frame," we might call it) in Luke's story that the painter has chosen to depict.[8] In the pages that follow you'll be invited to imagine Mary responding to Gabriel's call in many different states of mind—anxious, eager, cogitating, bemused, easy in spirit, frightened—along with commentary exploring why that particular rendering might have seemed especially compelling to the artist who created it, or to the patron who requested it, or to the people who would live with it.

Such variation might seem confusing—*Which one is right?*—but it's important to remember that *all* are, since they all record emotions that Luke reports Mary to have felt. Indeed, this variety was not just accepted but discussed approvingly in the period when these paintings were produced. The period's best-known classification of annunciation themes comes from a famous preacher, Fra Roberto Caracciolo of Lecce, who popularized terms for five stages in Mary's progress toward her *Magnificat*, educating the public on "the range of emotions that can be represented in a single moment of submission," in the words of critic John M. Carvalho. Such an approach coached citizens of the Renaissance in how to interpret contemporary paintings while simultaneously offering a framework for identifying their own inner states regarding obedience to God.[9]

A fundamental proposition of this book follows from that precedent. The art of the annunciation can still offer such a framework for us today, allowing us to acknowledge the variety of feelings that assail us as we grapple with saying "yes" to our own everyday annunciations, offering comfort through identification with this holy Mother who offers an at once peerless and relatable model in this process, as in all things . . . even as we acknowledge that her "Let it be done to me" was a lot quicker in coming than ours can ever hope to be.

An Invitation to Begin

Henri Nouwen's acclaimed *The Return of the Prodigal Son: A Story of Homecoming*—a book that helped inspire this one—provides a striking case study of how profound the results of communing with an image can be. In that book, Nouwen recounts how Rembrandt's painting of that iconic Bible parable (Luke 15:11-32) led him to put himself imaginatively into the place of each of its characters, and to research how Rembrandt might have been connecting with them consciously and unconsciously, given the artist's personal history. The sometimes uncomfortable insights into Nouwen's psyche which resulted from this exercise inspired in him seminal wisdom, allowing this troubled man to plumb his complex relationship with his father and with God, as well as his own capacities to judge and forgive.[10]

I hope this book's varied components, both paintings and words, will encourage you in a similarly honest way to "own" the variety of responses you have felt when some disturbing angel of circumstance has shown up on your own doorstep. I pray that bringing such personal history out into the light and turning it over as you read, reflect, and converse with God might afford tacit permission to be what you are—*human*—as you labor to reconcile yourself to the divine will.

Yes, sometimes it can seem difficult almost beyond possibility to imagine that what has happened to us might carry an invitation to move toward a meaningful new chapter of life. It might seem too hard a labor to transform loss into service. Yet I've come to believe that if we seek to live faithfully and fruitfully, we will have no choice but to embrace the changes that challenge us to begin anew, to employ our God-given creative powers in partnership with our Maker.

Let us begin, then, at the beginning, as a very young woman finds herself confronted by an exciting—though highly unusual—visitor . . .

Jacopo Pontormo, *The Annunciation*, 1527.

Chapter One

Early Annunciations

The Challenges of Youthful Vocation

How do I know you? One Saturday in early September of 2013, I was flipping through a pretty little book that compiled artists' renderings of the annunciation, marveling at the varied ways Mary's response has been depicted, beginning to imagine this book (and, frankly, playing hooky from the obligations of the final fall semester before my retirement), when one of the images held my gaze. What a beautiful, curious, extremely young Mary it depicted! How she stood out among all the devoutly dignified, pensive, anxious Marys on other pages!

Her half-smile suggests that this Mary, painted by Florentine artist Jacopo Pontormo in 1527, is hearing Gabriel's portentous announcement as an interesting surprise rather than worrying about its long-term import. She seems so relaxed and receptive, turning to face Gabriel, her gaze open and unafraid, her eyes looking directly into his instead of pensively downward. One arm is loose at her side, the other draped casually over a piece of furniture; her posture is full of dynamic energy rather than frozen in static contemplation. It's possible to imagine her breaking into that famous, beautiful song of praise at any moment. The angel appears to assume this youthful spirit himself, his head tilted to one side in a friendly way, his body similarly at ease with arms relaxed, body turning toward Mary rather than formally posed in a conventional gesture of announcement. They might be two teenagers companionably greeting each other in a school hallway, full of the youthful optimism that assumes only good things lie ahead.

Why did she seem so familiar? The obvious answer that day, revealed in the caption's small print, was that I'd seen this image in person in Florence, adorning a side chapel of the Church of Santa Felicita where I'd attended daily Mass. As a widow in the fall of 2004, I'd lingered alone in that church for hours, gazing around the quiet, dark space, struggling to connect with God in prayer.

Still, I couldn't shake the feeling that there was more to this recognition, some association more recent, more immediate. Just a few hours later (after I'd stopped trying to make the connection, of course) I understood: in affect as well as appearance, this Mary might have been the twin of Molly, a graduate student enrolled in the teaching practicum I was supervising that semester—one so excited about the experience that she'd stopped by my office several times before the semester even began, introducing herself, asking questions, chatting about teaching.

How enthusiastic Molly was to start her career in teaching, and how idealistic! From her girlhood Molly had delighted in love for the written word, and she'd dreamed with such fervor of passing on that love that she'd fought for the chance. Molly's sociable, sunny personality and can-do enthusiasm as a teen had led high school counselors to suggest that she choose a field like marketing or public relations; her parents had worried that an academic life of reading, writing, and teaching would not allow her "to make a good living like you could doing something practical." But all of those mentors were loving and recognized Molly's gifts, and ultimately, they granted their blessings for her to pursue her dreams. She got off to a good start, becoming a star undergraduate English major at the small Christian college she attended, and a young peer-teacher of great promise.

As a master's student, Molly radiated enthusiasm for what she believed to be her foreordained vocation. Commendably, she acknowledged that she had a lot to learn, and she wasn't quite sure how early days with her first ever class of freshman composition students would play out. But she'd been anticipating this "start of real life" for so many years and with so much joy, dreaming of the time when she'd finally get the chance to change students' lives as her teachers had changed hers, to introduce them to the riches of human thought. During the semester's first teaching seminar meeting, she went so far as to adopt the language of faith in a secular setting, enthusing about how exciting it would be to "convert" those who hadn't yet learned to appreciate the beauty of arts and letters.

Mentally superimposing Molly's image onto Pontormo's Mary, I tasted again the boundless optimism that had once gripped me as a young teacher, when I too had dreamed about how I might change my students' lives for the better, how the happy ripple effect of my mentoring might echo down the generations of their students-to-be.

Nevertheless, as Molly's mentor, my heart ached a little, for, decades along in my work of guiding novice teachers, it was impossible not to anticipate the disappointing reality that would soon break over her head when she discovered that many of her students weren't quite so fascinated with reading and writing as she assumed they'd be. Neither would my own pedagogical road ahead likely be smooth, for if the previous cohorts of new teachers with whom I'd worked were any predictor, I knew that soon I'd be talking young idealists off ledges, witnessing rants and tears, offering lots of extra logistical help. I might even find myself mothering one or two as they realized that "generations of students-to-be" were decidedly *not* in their futures after all, and that what lay ahead instead was radical rethinking about what they were supposed to be doing with their lives.

The Joy of Youthful Calling

Such grizzled veteran spoil-sporting aside, there's no doubt that it's a glorious thing to be a young person who feels summoned by divine fiat to a particular life path. To be able to say, "This is what I'm meant to be!" is to quiet the weighty questions about identity and purpose that plague so many adolescents and young adults, and to be able to daydream about the future in specific, happy detail. Encouraged by evidence of individual gifts and talents, bolstered by others' reinforcement and by successful experiences, such a young person will naturally feel reverence, gratitude, even awe at being "chosen" for the particular vocation in question—anointed, as it were.

From a classic Catholic perspective, everybody has the potential to be in that position, formed in our mothers' wombs with distinctive capacities that prepare us for a unique "path of holiness," as Pope Francis has said, and thus fitted to play our part in the universal symphony that is the church and world.[1] St. Paul assures believers that "to each individual the manifestation of the Spirit is given for some benefit," inviting them to think of themselves metaphorically as body parts with distinct missions depending on their gifts, each essential for the life of the whole (1 Cor 12:4-31). One of the greatest spiritual advisors the church has ever known, St. Francis de Sales, also emphasized that God does guide individual paths to mission, writing that each Christian is called to pursue the "heart's desire" that the divine has placed inside of him or her, carefully "examin[ing] its condition, correcting and improving it" throughout the course of a life.[2]

So it's natural that devout and idealistic young people look forward with great enthusiasm to self-actualization in God's service. Those who imagine themselves created for working with others in a service occupation, like Molly, spin airy castles about how they'll change others' lives and better society. Those pulled to religious vocation might imagine a clear path of perfect faith and tireless service. Those who sense that they will contribute to the coming of God's kingdom through their marriages may paint mental pictures of lifelong accord, fulfillment, and unconditional support. As parenthood approaches, mothers and fathers might imagine raising loving, faithful children in a family whose unity will last forever and whose support for each other will influence the wider world for good.[3]

If they're young people who have joined Catholic youth groups and campus ministries, such enthusiasm might be reinforced by sharing their annunciation stories and learning about the vocation stories of the heroes of the church. Having spoken to such groups in my own parish and as a writer-in-residence at various universities and schools, I can attest that ears perk up when young people realize that God has often tapped young adults for noble service. You can almost literally see their idealism shining more brightly as they hear the tales of trust. They nod in recognition at stories of "coincidences" that turned young servants of God in the right direction—St. Ignatius of Loyola, for example, a bellicose young soldier who converted after finding literature on the saints in his sickroom after being wounded; and St. Frances Xavier Cabrini, who longed from childhood to be a missionary to China but was directed (against her will) by the church hierarchy to serve Catholic immigrants in America, to glorious effect.

In fact, if you're ever meeting with Catholic young people and need a conversation starter, let me suggest that inviting testimony concerning such personal "holy happenstances" is a perfect way to get things going. You might hear about chance meetings or missed flights that set someone on the right path, about undesired tasks that revealed unexpected affinity for a particular kind of service, about a mentor who felt heaven-sent to help a person find her way. If my experience is any predictor, by session's end all will be marveling at how inventive God can be at working through people and events in our lives when he's interested in guiding us down a particular path.

And I'll admit that I too felt such heady in-reaching as a young person, though nobody in the Presbyterian church I attended ever asked me to talk about it. In the case of my vocation as a writer, the prompting manifested itself through innate affinity and encouraging events. Among my earliest memories is filling in a drawing tablet with the looping swirls of pretend writing. I remember it as an instinctive, irresistible impulse, and I yielded to the pull so enthusiastically that every page had been "written on" in about fifteen minutes (much to the chagrin of my mother, who'd expected it to occupy my 3-year-old self for days). When I was in elementary school, teachers submitted my poems to the local weekly newspaper, which dutifully published them. High school teachers encouraged me; a friend's mother who appeared to me to be the epitome of arty sophistication praised my work, and before long it was being accepted for broader publication.

In the case of university teaching, I can identify the very day I was spun around and pointed in the right direction. One afternoon in 1969, one of my professors at the University of Delaware summoned me to her office for a paper review. The only female full professor in the department, then in her fifties and favoring old-fashioned wool skirt suits and sensible shoes, she had a reputation for "telling it like it is," as we used to say in those days, so this one-on-one wasn't something I'd anticipated with pleasure. Sure enough, the session began sternly as she admonished me, "You must do something about your spelling" (not news to me in that pre-spellcheck era, but hearing it stung). Then she paused, looked chastened me straight in the eye, and, breaking into a beaming smile, announced that I "simply *must* go to graduate school."

At the time I was only vaguely aware that such a thing as graduate school existed and possessed only a fuzzy sense of what it entailed, since, as the middle-class daughter of a CPA father and homemaker mother, I knew no one except my professors who'd been. But I was well aware that Dr. Anna Janey DeArmond *never* said anything she didn't mean. That afternoon's routine conference, in an ordinary campus office with autumn sunlight slanting in through the windows, first planted the seed that grew into four decades of rich, challenging, sometimes maddening, always heart-delighting vocation as a college professor. I shiver every time I remember that afternoon, grateful for the goodness of a God who led me to that frank and generous mentor . . . that sterling Gabriel surrogate.

The creator of that eager young Madonna whose image anchors this chapter, artist Jacopo Pontormo, himself experienced an extraordinary case of apparent divine in-reaching—a case that makes mine look positively bland. Born in 1494 in a suburb of Florence, the young Pontormo could not have dreamed that a career as an eminent artist lay ahead, even if he'd sensed his own talent. As a working-class boy he was destined to follow in his father's and grandfather's shoemaking occupation. Then tragedy intervened. Pontormo's father died when he was just five years old, his mother when he was ten, and his grandfather three years later. With no one left at home to teach him his trade, the young boy was dispatched to a relative's cobbler workshop in the city. Soon after, his loving grandmother and his sister each died, leaving Pontormo an orphan devoid of nurturing connections.

But then something unexpected happened. Still in his teens, the boy was plucked from the shoemaker's employ and placed as an assistant in a minor artist's workshop, then in a slightly more prestigious one, then in a series of better-known artists' work-shops.[4] Thus he was launched into a creative future. It appears that a talent-spotter had noticed artistic promise in this shoemaker's apprentice, convinced his master to free him from his contract, and talked an artist into offering the boy a chance.

Given this sudden redirection of his life and career, it might not be an accident that Pontormo's first known work was a "tiny Annunciation" he painted for a friend. Even if he chose the subject simply because of its popularity with contemporary artists at the time, an inescapable sign of his calling soon followed, when the influential Renaissance artist Raphael of Urbino somehow came across that tiny Annunciation on a visit to Florence. "When he saw the painting and the young man who had executed it," art historian Giorgio Vasari writes, Raphael was "completely astonished" and "predicted for Jacopo the success he was later to achieve."

That acclaim was only the beginning. Not one to miss a chance in the talent-spotting department, the great Florentine artist Andrea del Sarto summoned Pontormo as a formally indentured apprentice. Now Pontormo was not just mixing paints and helping set up scaf-folding but was delegated to fill in subsections of large frescoes. One such effort, involving two figures in an alcove at the Church of the Annunciation (Are you getting chills at the pattern of reference?) inspired "immense astonishment and wonder" in his teacher and triggered another "anointing" from none other than Michaelangelo himself. "This young man will be such an artist," that great master proclaimed, "that if he lives and continues on, he will exalt this art to the heavens."

By the time Pontormo painted that wide-eyed, responsive Mary, he'd been heading his own workshop for a decade, building the reputation that inspired the painting's commission by those who directed Santa Felicita. No longer a humble shoemaker-to-be, he now worked on that church's remodeling alongside one of Florence's most prominent artists, the architect Brunelleschi, famous for designing the city's remarkable domed cathedral. It's no wonder, then, that the Mary imagined by Pontormo for Santa Felicita seems so willing, so unafraid to undertake the assignment offered to her. Plucked from obscurity by a series of events so incredible that it must have felt like destiny, at 33 the man who held the brush might have been painting himself, recording the glorious, almost giddy sense a person feels when the universe (or God) confirms his ability and purpose.

Encountering Vocational Challenges

If only the highs of our early callings could last! If only accepting a summons to vocation meant riding unbroken waves of happy fulfillment as spouses, parents, consecrated religious, and practitioners of particular occupations. Yet the sort of perfect, lifelong fit Pontormo felt with his vocation is rare indeed. In the vast majority of cases (and in saints' lives, too, if that's any consolation), even the most welcome calling will likely evolve over time.

It is possible, of course, that the troubles of "fit" a person feels early on in her vocation, if severe and persistent enough, might just indicate that she has made a mistake about her calling, particularly if utilitarian motives played a major role in the choice

("Everybody in my family is a doctor" or "I'd like to make good money without working too hard"), or if the choice was based on a misapprehension of the vocation's nature ("Most of what lawyers do is make dramatic speeches"). It's also possible to have inadequately assessed one's own gifts, as occurred for several young participants in the massage therapy training program I pursued after retiring (see chapters 3 and 4). Despite romantically believing themselves to be "natural healers" destined to holistically change lives, these 18-year-olds discovered to their frustration and sorrow that they either lacked the discipline necessary to grasp the lessons in anatomy, physiology, and kinesiology required for passing the national qualifying test, or that they were too shy to communicate effectively with clients or unwilling to take the direction required of beginners in the health professions. Soon, sad to say, they were forced to consider other ways of making a living.

More unfortunately still, some people don't seem to realize that the vocation they've chosen is wrong for them until they're well-settled into its practice. Perhaps you've encountered a young doctor who, though proficient in book learning, proves chronically unwilling to listen, or perhaps your child's teacher, though very caring, appears terminally disorganized and incapable of maintaining classroom discipline. In such cases an observer of goodwill can only hope that—unless the individual digs deep to acquire the necessary skills—sooner or later the wake-up calls of chronically poor evaluations, lost business, sullied relationships, anxiety, or simply daily reluctance to go to work, will inspire ground-up rethinking about what she is supposed to be doing with her life. Until that occurs, the situation is not going to be optimal for that person, those with whom she interacts, or for God's intentions, to say the least.

Yet a person shouldn't be too ready to throw in the towel, for even the truest of callings is likely to involve a steep learning curve once its daily realities hit home, as that paragon of spiritual advisors, St. Francis de Sales, recognized hundreds of years ago. Counseling those who might have become too easily discouraged, too quickly dissuaded by the natural difficulties of a valid vocation, he writes that "a firm and constant will to serve God" is a good indication of a true calling, but then goes on to say, "I do not mean that from the very beginning [the person starting a vocation] would do everything that is necessary [in its practice] . . . with such a firmness and constancy of will that she is free of all repugnance, difficulty or distaste. . . . No, I do not mean that; still less that this firmness and constancy of will be such that she is devoid of committing faults, nor so strong that she would never waver or falter in the undertaking she has taken on herself."[5]

In other words, "you don't have to 100% love your job from the start in order for it to be your destiny," as a career counselor once advised a young friend of mine. From a Christian perspective, what you *do* have to do if you suspect the fit might be wrong, before you even start to think about quitting, is to park your panic, adjust your expectations, ask God to lead and counsel you aright, and seek a spiritual advisor or a career counselor. You also need to commit to acquiring the skills and personal capacities that are necessary for the vocation you've chosen, even if those skills initially seem beyond your own intellectual, psychological, spiritual, or even physical makeup.

Such was the challenge my sweet Molly faced, just as I'd feared. Before the semester's first month was out, this idealist found her sense of calling seriously wobbling, tipped off its airy pedestal by the very students she'd been so eager to enlighten. As anyone who's worked with rookie teachers (or has been one) might anticipate, the problem grew not from her own carelessness or ill intentions but from naivete about the vocation's reality. In Molly's case that naivete involved assuming that others' experiences of learning would be like her own. Based on the undergraduate honors classes she herself had enjoyed, Molly assumed that intense discussions and lively participation was the norm for college classrooms. What she witnessed in her own class, however, could hardly have been more different.

The disillusionment came soon since, in an apparent indication that the universe has a nasty sense of humor, the lottery of scheduling that semester dealt Molly a particularly indifferent—aggressively indifferent, it's fair to say—bunch of students. Freshman composition was for these students a gratuitous burden imposed by an out-of-touch university, a hurdle to surmount on the way to the "real world." They couldn't imagine any way that writing could help them in their careers, much less improve their minds. They insisted they "just weren't any good at writing" and made it abundantly clear that they believed this "exploring abstract ideas with words" thing was nothing but a touchy-feely, irrelevant frill.

There are plenty of effective ways to work with such students, of course, plenty of ways gradually to convince them of writing's relevance, plenty of teaching techniques that will help them enjoy success in pursuing it. But Molly—with her assumption that her students would be all-in from day one—hadn't imagined that she needed to learn such strategies, much less incorporate any into her syllabus. Without any policy in place to hold her students accountable for reading assignments, they naturally ignored them . . . and thus could not participate in discussions, much less initiate the insightful, flowing conversations Molly had imagined would characterize her classroom. Her classes devolved into question-and-answer "tennis" with two or three nice students who felt sorry for her. Attendance diminished. Students texted or played games on their devices while she talked. "They don't respect me *at all*," she wailed at a third-week conference, tearfully exhibiting a plagiarized paper a student had submitted for the first, easy assignment. "Of course they don't! I'm totally letting them down!" Intending to spare me the agony of imagining I'd have to mentor someone so hopeless for long, Molly assured me that she'd quit grad school at the semester's end and resign her teaching assistantship to somebody who was better qualified.

One of the best teachers I've ever met, a foundational mentor to me, would have diagnosed in Molly what he termed "Conductor's Disease," by which he meant the irrational belief that a leader is totally, utterly responsible for whether an enterprise involving other people succeeds. Certainly, a teacher has a pivotal effect on how a class responds, he'd acknowledge. But those being taught—that willful bunch of "musicians" metaphorically refusing to practice their violins or banging randomly on their timpani—have their own independent power to transform potential cooperative success into chaotic failure. They must shoulder their own responsibilities, or the enterprise will inevitably struggle.

In its least attractive manifestation, Conductor's Disease is fueled by pure egotism—*As the smartest one here, I call the shots, and everybody else should bow to my authority.* One of Molly's classmates, an extremely bright but perfectionistic young woman, displayed an incurable case. Driven by the desire to demonstrate how brilliant she was, and by what she imagined as the prestige of being a college professor, she responded to her students' resistance with loathing. Thank heavens she left the profession after two awful semesters, extending as she did a parting look of pity toward the rest of her cohort, doomed to toil in these unpropitious fields.

Fortunately for Molly, her strain of Conductor's Disease had a different cause, grounded as it was in a laudable sense of personal responsibility. The frustration she felt with her dysfunctional classroom turned inward into guilt, not outward to her students. Knowing me to be a person of faith, she couldn't help but "confess" that sense of existential failure. "God trusted me to do this," she sobbed. "I know he did. I felt so inspired, so proud. But somehow, I fooled him. I'm a total, hopeless fraud, and he's got to be disgusted with me."

Not so fast, I reassured her, and she agreed to persevere. The weeks that followed included plenty of pep talks and training in classroom strategies, along with extra observations and private coaching sessions. Molly continued to lead our conversations in the direction of what might have been termed "amateur spiritual advising" on my part, and followed through with lots of prayer and reaching out to the God she feared was so disappointed in her. ("Don't slink around in shame, hiding!" I told her, repeating wisdom once passed on to me in the sacrament of reconciliation. "Now is *exactly* when you need to talk to him.") On her own initiative, Molly adopted Isaiah 41:10 as her mantra, meditating on it morning and evening, printing it out and keeping it on her desktop (and ignoring her office partners' raised eyebrows): "Do not fear: I am with you; do not be anxious: I am your God. I will strengthen you, I will help you."

Her vision of a perfect classroom brought down to earth, Molly granted that growing into a teaching vocation required her to face the hard truth that neither she nor her students were perfect, or ever would be. She cultivated patience regarding her own nature, laboring to accept that the mistakes she made didn't indicate incurable flaws of character or unsuitability for this calling, but opportunities for development. She opened in compassion to her students, asking them about their backgrounds and aspirations rather than assuming what they were like or why they were acting as they did, figuring out ways to meet them where they were. "They're all so different from each other, it turns out," she informed me a few weeks into this process with a shrug. "I should have known that. They're really interesting people, not just vessels to pour knowledge into." At the same time, she was gaining the confidence to "be the teacher" rather than the friendly, totally accepting facilitator she'd assumed her students wanted. I knew we'd crossed an important threshold when Molly requested tips for motivating students to submit assignments on time, remarking, "Love is not enough—I need to be strategic here!" Classroom discipline improved, as did the quality of her students' writing. By the semester's end, she'd even managed a handful of the "conversions" she'd hoped for—sort of.

The person most fundamentally changed during that semester, though, was Molly herself. She evolved from an impossibly idealistic child to a young woman of growing confidence—a woman with a tempered ego willing to admit she could use advice and support. Crucially, she'd become more capable of real charity now that she had acknowledged shortcomings as a common human denominator for everyone, including herself.

"It hasn't been pretty, but it's been good," she admitted in her final seminar class. "Actually, I learned more than my students."

Accepting God's Help

Though it can feel tempting to wail with Jeremiah, "You duped me, O God, and I let myself be duped" (20:7) when the realities of a much-anticipated vocation don't match our starry-eyed dreams, the fact is that God often works through these circumstances to help us grow in humility and discover capacities we didn't imagine our natures contained. The challenges of early vocation disabuse us of any sense that we're "special" children who can begin to control what happens to us. They teach us to turn to God as we discard any illusions of our own perfection; they invite us to refine our skills of discernment and pay attention to others' perspectives. Successfully navigated, they can even serve as baby-step practice in learning to cope with the more wrenching annunciations that maturity so often brings, providing undeniable evidence of our own resilience and teaching us that life is not over when our expectations must be modified.

It's some consolation, in fact, to realize that such experiences don't just happen to certain human beings, but to everybody (such challenges can be indications of God's love; they are not necessarily signs of divine exasperation). That's the prophet Jeremiah who's complaining above, after all. Moses himself did his share of shaking a fist at the sky (not to say whining) when the Israelites proved persistently rebellious during the journey to the Promised Land. Bernadette of Lourdes, an innocent child, could not have imagined that her vocation as witness to the Virgin Mary's visitation would set her up for painful trials—the dismissals, the accusations of credulity, ignorance, madness, and deliberate deception, the intrusive publicity. Servant of God Dorothy Day continued throughout her life to encounter obstacles as she worked to support the dignity of the poor and their economic stability—not just from hostile authorities, but also from some who lived on the cooperative farms and in the settlement houses she'd established.

We all go into our callings partially blind. That was even true for Mary, who was provided with only minimal, mysterious information at that original annunciation: that she would be "overshadowed" by

God and bear a son, Jesus, a great man who would ascend to David's throne and rule forever (Luke 1:30-36). Not long after her "yes," signs begin suggesting that the service she's signed up for is going to be more vexing than she might have imagined. Herod's wrath sends her little family fleeing to escape the murder of the innocents (Matt 2:13-18).[6] Simeon tells Mary directly that she will feel the piercing of a sword (Luke 2:35). She is "astonished" to find the child Jesus teaching in the temple (after experiencing "great anxiety" when she could not find him) and ponders what these things mean (Luke 2:48-51). Indeed, throughout Jesus' life, his mother must grapple with the unfolding of his mission and all it will entail.

Given all this, the answer to the question posed in the contemporary Christian song "Mary, Did You Know?" must be a simple and conclusive "no" regarding the specifics of Gabriel's announcement. But that's the theological point, right? It's precisely because Mary did not "know" the implications of the vocation to which she'd been invited, but nevertheless surrendered in absolute trust, that she stands as such a transcendent model of faith for the rest of us. It's not faith, after all, if there's a point-by-point contract spelled out.

All that's predictable when one heeds a calling and takes up a vocation, it seems, is that surprises *will* come, that our vocations may very well "sunfish out from under us" (to use a made-up verb from one of my husband's poems, indicating "to go sideways"), darting in a flash in unanticipated directions we don't expect and may not enjoy.

Directions, we can only trust, that can work for our own good, and the broader good, too.

A Case Study in Unfolding Vocation

At this writing Molly's story is still incomplete—though for the past two years she's been successfully teaching in a community college, gaining a reputation as an effective, beloved teacher, and thus cheering the hopes of all who love her. To illustrate what shape a full-term version of ongoing listening/heeding/growing in a vocation might take—the process I pray Molly enjoys, and one I hope this book helps you embrace, too—let me give you an example of how idealistic aspirations, necessary learning, and creative attentiveness to what could be interpreted as God's "pestering" led to an exemplary life, indeed.

This story concerns the beautiful soul Sr. Bernadette Stang, a Benedictine sister at the Monastery of St. Gertrude in Cottonwood, Idaho, who died a few years ago at age 85. Like Molly, Bernadette felt a strong early calling to a particular kind of service to God and others—in her case, to a vocation as a religious sister. From her serious, pious girlhood in a German-Catholic community in rural Minnesota, Bernadette had dreamed of being a nun. An obituary written by her religious sisters identifies the favorite Bible verse of her childhood as the rather somber Matthew 16:26, which speaks of losing the world to gain the soul. When she was 21, Bernadette traveled to Idaho to visit her aunts who had professed at St. Gertrude's and immediately recognized this particular monastery as the place she was supposed to live out her vocation. Soon she made her first profession, describing herself as "happier than I had ever been before."

Even with certainty about her calling, however, Bernadette soon realized that becoming a Benedictine sister wasn't going to be easy, especially given her personality. Though deeply devout, Bernadette had exhibited an opinionated streak and high spirits from girlhood, a temperament out of keeping with monastery decorum of the time. It soon became evident that she was given to joking and (as the staid older nuns termed it) "romping." While glowing with youthful idealism during the ceremonial rites of passage—having her head shaven, donning the heavy habit with its wimple—Bernadette found the pre-Vatican II monastic discipline grating ("Especially the silence—can you imagine me silent all day long?").

The strict routine of chores expected of women in formation in those days also proved a trial. "I'd been expecting to impress everybody by gladly suffering temptations and terrible demonic trials, like some latter-day Little Flower," Bernadette self-deprecatingly told me with a grin. "Now here I was working every day at the kind of housekeeping chores I'd had to do at home but on a much bigger scale, plus working in the gardens and with the farm animals. I thought, 'Anybody could do this! This isn't religious vocation! This is slave labor!' And I wasn't getting *any* sleep, and I hated being ordered around like I was nobody."

Bernadette's discontent came to a head one day when, after spilling a big pail of dirty water as she mopped the refectory floor (the task itself assigned as a reproof for some previous careless mishap at her duties), she was physically disciplined in a way she would only describe to me as "very harsh." Even this humiliation, however, didn't quell her spirits, and during a meeting with the mother superior, she complained bitterly of the unfairness of that treatment in particular and of the treatment of novices in general, offering what she described as "way more than my two cents" on how she thought religious life should operate.

"Well, you haven't made your final profession yet," the mother superior remarked, breaking the extended, heavy silence that followed Bernadette's tirade. "Maybe this is a sign that you don't belong here. Maybe you should go back to Minnesota."

"I can't go anywhere," Bernadette wailed. "I don't have any *HAIR!*"

"So, it was vanity," this spiritual mentor of mine confessed with a smile forty years later as we sat in the cool of her pretty office, the summer sun outside coaxing those still-vital gardens toward fruition, "Vanity that made me stay here." I smiled at the exaggeration, understanding that what had really kept Bernadette at St. Gertrude's was determined faith and an intentional process of discernment, one that taught her to trust that, although different from what she'd expected, religious life was indeed the path to which her Heavenly Father was calling her.

She returned my smile as peace filled the room. We spoke of the rich life's work that her "staying" had made possible—as a novice mistress herself, a spiritual director, a parish and hospital administrator, a missionary to South America, the monastery's retreat center director. So many young sisters, catechists, and re-treatants had seen in Bernadette evidence that quirkiness, questioning, and individuality are not incompatible with faith or community—an essential lesson for spirited souls of all stripes who dream of serving God.

Among the most striking of Bernadette's calling-within-a-calling stories occurred well after that rocky beginning, when she reached her late forties. The incident which prompted her rethinking involved a car accident that killed the priest friend with whom Bernadette was riding, and seriously injured her. She believed, she told me, that she didn't die because there was some work God still wanted her to do. Within a few weeks a dream (now there's a classic everyday annunciation!) led Bernadette to believe she was being called to transition from her current nursing vocation to work with the oppressed. Receiving permission, encouragement, and donations, Bernadette went on to establish an after-school outreach program for children and women at a Hispanic migrant farmworkers' camp near the community where she'd been a nurse . . . a community, it can unfortunately be said, where the migrants' presence had only been tolerated as a labor-resource necessity. Still thriving many decades later, that program has afforded dignity and fun, access to social services, as well as programs in the arts, music, American culture, and English language. Children who in its absence might have had very few options have received scholarships, earned higher education degrees, and become nurses, doctors, teachers, labor organizers, and employees of our diocese.

"God seduces us, pure and simple," this soul-friend proclaimed to me with trademark wisdom. "We love him and we trust him, so we buy in, and then boy, does he beckon us onto unexpected paths! And how unfair what he sends us seems sometimes! But in the end, we have to remember that God will use even the things we can't understand and don't like for good if we let him—even if the process isn't pretty, even if we have doubts along the way."

I miss Bernadette-in-the-flesh so much . . . though I remain convinced that she must be gloriously happy in the afterlife, and that, if there is anyone I've known personally who deserves to join the communion of saints—not just in a general sense but in an official, capital letter one—she does.

✦ ✦ ✦

"Seduction" might seem like an odd word to use in reference to God, or an odd word for a nun to employ at all. But I've loved it ever since Bernadette voiced it. With its implication of irresistible attraction proffered by God—the divine "bait" tailored individually, perfectly, to hook (even to "dupe"!) us in our idealism—that word characterizes so well the heady give-and-take of a vocation's dawning. And it is the sustaining joy (as Dorothy Day insisted her vocation offered, despite all its vexations) that can buoy us on long after early struggles have disrupted initial daydreams.

It's a great move on God's part to set that hook hard at the beginning, you have to admit. For if we once turned in curious, rapt, open-hearted, fearless fascination toward what seemed to be a joyously holy future, we're unlikely to forget that initial heady thrill. We're likely, in fact, to hug it to our hearts as reassurance when troubles threaten to shake our faith regarding the whole enterprise of serving God.

Even witnessing in someone else such an overarching sense of joyful calling—a shining confidence that "the Mighty One has done great things for me" (Luke 1:49, *Magnificat*)—can inspire others, too, to seek, refine, and reaffirm their own God-intended vocations. Who wouldn't want some of that, after all?

Such a thing recently happened to me, in fact, on the day of a funeral of a physician in my parish who devoted her maturity to working with elderly patients. Observing a need for eldercare in our region that was greater than she alone could address, she founded a home health and hospice practice with a very long reach indeed, one where compassion and patient-first ethics were valued above profits. Generations of nurses, CNAs, care aids, therapists, social workers, and doctors have been shaped by her enlightened philosophy of geriatric care (including me, after she hired me to work with her patients).

Dr. Morris's patients didn't just respect and trust her; they adored her. I once encountered an elderly woman among them who grinned the widest smile imaginable at the mention of this doctor's name. She regaled me not only with an account of the attentive, loving care Dr. Morris had provided for her dying husband, but also spoke with gratitude of the day in 2021 when, after our community had run out of Covid vaccines, this physician had used her personal time and vehicle to drive some of her elderly patients and their caregivers to a distant city where shots were still available. She'd just wanted to be sure that all of her patients and their family caregivers who wanted to be protected would be, she'd assured them, as though it were no big deal.

Dr. Morris died too early, in her late sixties, of pancreatic cancer, leaving behind dear friends, a devoted husband and daughter, a brand-new granddaughter, and beautiful memories of good works. The funeral, as you might expect, was packed, but despite their sadness, few seemed absolutely disconsolate. She'd lived a rich, full life, everyone agreed, and there was no doubt about her strong Catholic faith. In fact, she'd been a leader on the parish council and a major force in obtaining the resources and funds necessary to repair and restore the historic chapel where that very Mass was held. Thus it felt fitting that the priest's sweet and respectfully funny homily, the loving stories being shared, and the mix of Dr. Morris's friends from different spheres encountering each other to their happy surprise, all made her funeral feel like a "celebration of life" to an extent that term rarely describes.

I couldn't attend the luncheon afterwards, for massage appointments with five of her medical group's hospice patients filled my schedule that afternoon. But as I drove across town toward the first nursing home on the day's list, Dr. Morris stayed so lovingly on my mind, and my prayers flowed, too—prayers of gratitude for her care for others, and of thanksgiving for her shepherding me at the start of my second-act career with the elderly and dying. One of the hymns we'd just sung kept playing in my mind—Donna Marie McGargill's "Servant Song," whose lyrics perfectly captured how Dr. Morris had lived her faith:

> *What do you want of me, Lord?*
> *Where do you want me to serve you?*
> *Where can I sing your praises?*
> *I am your song.*[7]

Let those words be mine today too, as a living tribute to her, I prayed as I turned off the engine and gathered my things and my focus in preparation for the afternoon's first session. *Let me be your song this afternoon.*

In that moment I was more than a decade along in my "new" vocation as a hospice massage therapist, far from a bright young thing, far from a naive idealist. I'd done enough such work to have accepted that people sometimes rejected my touch, and that on occasion the work of my hands failed to comfort them. I also knew, though, that more often than not my modest efforts *did* change their days for the better—relaxing tight muscles, easing headaches, calming the panicked, inviting the restless to peaceful sleep at least for a while.

May such things happen by your grace today, I prayed as I stepped from the car . . . turning toward the angel of calling, my spirit dancing at the day's possibilities.

Lorenzo Lotto, *The Annunciation*, ca. 1534.

Chapter Two

Annunciations that Change Everything

The Fraught and Holy Path toward Acceptance

The young woman in the painting propels herself away from those intruding on her quiet domestic space, agitation obvious in her garments' twisting swirl. Her eyes are wide open and staring. Her arms are raised in what one art historian has termed a "defensive" gesture, her posture described as an "attempt to distance herself from . . . her destiny."[1] Hunched over, she looks directly at viewers, perhaps imploring them to do something about what's happening. Behind her a pet cat also tries to escape the interlopers, its arched back and fluffed hair suggesting terror—reading and mirroring its owner's mood, as devoted cats are apt to do.

And such agitation is no wonder, given the daunting nature of those who have thrust themselves into her world, utterly surprising, even shocking her. God the Father vigorously approaches from the enclosed garden beyond the room; the leading edge of the attendant cloud is at that moment breaking the plane of the porch, intruding into her private domestic space. Gabriel has already entered the room, standing with an assertively, even confrontationally, direct gaze; his muscular, raised arm suggests command/

39

demand rather than invitation. His shadow is advancing toward the young woman though she's clearly not yet agreed to be "overshadowed," his assertive energy disturbing a once-serene realm.

As you'll have guessed, the young woman in the painting is Mary, specifically Mary as imagined by northern Italian painter Lorenzo Lotto around 1534 in a work painted for a guildhall in a town northeast of Rome. If you're used to imagining Mary as unruffled in her acquiescence, Lotto's work, known as the *Recanati Annunciation*,[2] might even shock you, for he takes considerable liberty in imagining how "greatly troubled" might have appeared.

Though I once imagined Fra Angelico's 1432 San Marco fresco an outlier in its approach, in actuality its depiction of Mary's anxiety falls somewhere in the middle of the spectrum of contemporary Annunciation paintings that depict Mary's moment of disquiet or *conturbatio* to employ the term used by Renaissance art theory to identify this freeze-frame in Luke's narrative (see introduction, note 9). Some artists who choose this disquiet as their subject matter imagine the Virgin as merely worried and confused, including Girolamo Mazzola Bedoli, whose sixteenth-century triptych altarpiece imagines the Madonna as momentarily disoriented when interrupted at her reading. Others suggest a somewhat greater degree of discomfort (see Simone Martini's 1333 Mary, who shrinks away, scowling). And Lotto is far from unique among Renaissance artists in his depiction of an actively resisting Mary. In Sandro Botticelli's 1489 *Cestello Annunciation* and Carlo Braccesco's 1490 painting of the same subject, Mary appears to be vigorously fending off Gabriel.[3]

Some Catholic writers have looked askance at renderings of the annunciation that emphasize Mary's initial discomfort, suggesting that to invite contemplation of this particular freeze-frame in Luke's story misrepresents her. ("Art tends not to *get* Mary," one complained recently.[4]) Yet it would be a mistake to imagine such representations as presumptive evidence of their creators' weak faith, misunderstanding of Mary, or desire to undermine others' belief. Many who chose this theme in the Renaissance era were renowned in their own period as people of great religious devotion, including Fra Angelico, a monk whom contemporaries speculated must have been in direct contact with God to paint as divinely as he did. Lorenzo Lotto was himself reportedly a man of prayer and regular religious observance, not someone who would have been interested in subverting others' reverence for Mary or Scripture.

Moreover, the historical moment in which Lotto painted his rather panicking Madonna would have been a particularly inauspicious one for a Catholic artist to have intentionally created a theologically "edgy" work (especially an artist who often relied on ecclesiastical patronage, as Lotto did). At that point in church history the standards of orthodoxy were tightening for artists. As the Council of Trent debated and published an official Catholic response to the Protestant Reformation, among its prominent concerns was Protestant iconoclasm. Affirming that Catholic art should above all teach and bolster faith, the Council established standards for such artistic productions, forcefully condemning works that were fanciful, self-indulgently mannered, or, most importantly, that threatened to mislead the faithful.[5] It's thus hard to imagine that Lotto would have jeopardized his career by picturing what he believed to be heterodox.

It seems much more likely that Lotto understood himself as simply doing what his Renaissance peers understood themselves to be doing: inviting viewers to imagine themselves in the sacred scene and engaging their faith in a reflective, fruitful way. Emphasizing human dignity and freedom, the period's dominant classical-humanist creative theory held that those who "consumed" artistic productions should not just admire them but should draw from them greater knowledge of self, others, and, in the case of religious art, God. Such context is crucial for "reading" this painting in a way appropriate for its time and place, as is the fact that the scene Lotto depicted in his *Recanati Annunciation* would have been understood by the period's Christians as a brief prologue to the story's next episode, in which this frightened and resisting woman does muster her courage and faith, and surrenders willingly.

Lotto's work has recently prompted me to reflect on the work of contemporary theologian Elizabeth Johnson, who argues that Mary's nature as a woman who "lived through the common human lot" of suffering, wondering, and struggling is as important to faith formation as her unique quality of being born without original sin. Only when Mary is "no longer the exception but rather the rule," only when we can recognize that she bears a human nature like ours, Johnson writes, can Mary become "a figure with trans-formational power"—someone who acts as a model, encouraging us to reach beyond what we believe is our own capacity regarding God. In the case of Lotto's painting, that process might translate to viewers imagining how they, like Mary, might successfully traverse the often fraught, real-life process of accepting God's will (even if they're among those who exaggerate, intensify, and prolong the "How can this be?" part beyond its biblical timeframe).

While my research has not unearthed any evidence that Lotto's own life provided inspiration for the admittedly "extreme" level of resistance depicted in his Annunciation, the Fra Angelico painting discussed earlier in this book itself provides an intriguing (though admittedly speculative) case study of how a *conturbatio* rendering of Luke's account might address themes of disquiet/obedience in a way vitally relevant to the specific circumstances of artist/ intended viewers.

Consider, to begin, the fact that this fresco was created in a place that called for an especially important and ever-relevant theme, a spot where Fra Angelico's community would see it regularly at the top of the grand staircase at San Marco which connected the foundation's common space with its dormitory rooms for individual clerics, lay brothers, and novices. Every single day, the members of that Dominican community would have descended that staircase to worship and observe the Liturgy of the Hours in the chapel, to fulfill their assigned work or learning, to eat together in the refec-tory. Then, as they climbed those steps again to return to their cells, the image would have loomed above their heads, inviting their eyes.

While Mary's annunciation is certainly an important theme in and of itself, it can be argued that Fra Angelico's particular "take" involving disquiet would have borne particular relevance for these monks, who would have been—people being people—themselves exposed to nagging temptations and moments of doubt. During the hours between descending those stairs and climbing them again, the holy duties in which they engaged inevitably would have been touched by the sort of frictions that are universal among those who make their lives together in families and communities. Those Dominicans might have found their patience tested on a particular day, for instance, by others who didn't perform their housekeeping or liturgical duties with competence. A perception of favoritism could have tempted them to jealousy. Even small tensions had the potential to introduce disharmony into community life and might have tainted an individual's sense of vocation—especially if the friar in question was also suffering the simple boredom, self-doubt, and dark nights of the soul so often reported in monastic autobiography. "This isn't what I expected," such a friar might have privately complained, as my friend Bernadette did centuries later . . . or might have even begun to daydream about fleeing this way of life.

Fra Angelico was a man familiar with such realities of community life (he'd been a monk for years at the time that fresco was created), a man who would have understood that at least some of his confreres were likely struggling to make peace with their lot. What better way to address discouragement and disaffection than to remind them that "even Mary" had not been exempt from anxiety and doubt on the path God had set before her, but that she nevertheless drew on her faith and courage to stay true to the vocation to which she'd been called?

Mary was, moreover, uniquely affiliated with the life of this community, for the Dominicans at San Marco were deeply devoted to her. Indeed, the monastery's daily routines ensured that Mary was ever-before the monks' eyes in not just a literal sense, but in the figurative sense of ritual. Each day the monks' liturgical observances included saying the Little Office of the Blessed Virgin Mary; they also sang the "Salve Regina" daily during a procession to an altar devoted to Mary. Thus they actively cultivated what the art historian William Hood has termed an "intense but poetically affective identification with what they imagined to have been the psychology of the Virgin Mary."[6]

So maybe I was simply reinventing a well-worn wheel of spiritual reassurance on that afternoon in 2004 when I myself identified with Fra Angelico's Mary. If so, I hope that somewhere, in the ebullient part of heaven where artists beloved of God enjoy their eternity, Fra Angelico noticed and approved.

Change as a Commonality of Human Life

As I work on this chapter (fittingly, today marks the feast of the Annunciation, 2023), I can think of specific contemporaries of mine who would also benefit from having such a message of encouragement inscribed where they could see it every single day. An epidemic of change is sweeping through my acquaintances at the moment, as if the fall of one domino of imagined security has somehow begun a chain reaction. Cancer has returned in a woman whose lymphedema I've been treating for a decade, a twenty-year survivor who considered herself cured. A social media acquaintance has lost her father, her bulwark. A young widow has been fired from her dream job as an educator, her sole means of supporting her children. Another young woman has dropped a bombshell on her mother, who is also my massage client: given spousal abandonment and foreclosure, she and her four young children have no choice but to return home to live. "I love them so, but the only place for them to sleep is my living room," my friend laments. "How are we ever going to cope?"

Closest to the bone of all—for it echoes something that might soon happen in my own family, or in anyone's family, really—are the circumstances of my neighbor's mother Margaret and sister Ellen. Having resided for several years in a sunny, memento-filled assisted-living suite, Margaret's about to learn that after yet another fall and a steadily accumulating list of health problems, she's destined to move to a small hospital-style room in that facility's skilled nursing wing.

It's not that Margaret's unprepared for weathering change. Her life has been full of upheavals, including divorce from an abusive husband, returning to work and building a successful career, retiring to a life full of involvement in women's service clubs, continuing education, and travel. As her health began to fail several years ago, she freely agreed to move into the suite she now occupies, entering with interest into her facility's activities and making new friends.

This change, though, will cut more deeply than any of those others, compromising the independence Margaret has so cherished. Her privacy will be interrupted by nurses and aides moving often through her room to help with the activities of daily living and to monitor her vital statistics. Her freedom to wander on a whim down to the common area for conversation, a communal jigsaw puzzle, or cards will be dependent on the availability of helpers, medical schedules, and her daily condition. Somebody else will be deciding what she does, and when, from now on.

Less obvious but no less wrenching are the upheavals facing Margaret's daughter Ellen, who is having difficulty accepting Margaret's decline. She'll soon be challenged to rebuild her life—and her self-defining role as their mother's best friend and primary caregiver—from the ground up once she's not required to run to the nursing home each day to provide companionship, groceries, and health check-ins.

"How will they cope?" my neighbor asks, her face troubled.

How foolish I was during those years immediately following Ford's death, when I believed that there had never been any sorrow like my sorrow, any grief like my grief! How unimaginably self-absorbed. For I was, after all, only experiencing what legions have experienced through the ages, were then experiencing alongside me, are experiencing as you read this sentence . . . and what you may be experiencing right now.

The Natural Temptation to Say "No"

"Yes" is such a short word, such a seemingly simple word. Yet it's often such a difficult word to say. When the summons to unwelcome change portends an upset of everything that seems to matter most, making peace with it can feel beyond human capacity.

Such are the cases where a contemporary expression of extreme "no!" is apt to bloom. Those experiencing such disruptions can experience depression or breakdowns that make a constructive response impossible; conversely, they might keep reassuring everyone that they're just fine. Some futilely attempt to cling to old patterns; others engage in "magical thinking," imagining that denial might somehow restore the "old normal," or that the summons to change will turn out to be a false alarm. Others fall into addiction, or daydream about suicide or "accidents" that would make their struggle moot.

Another response—one that pretty much *all* of us mere mortals try for at least a little while, even if we're simultaneously whirling away in alarm—is the attempt to understand *why* the painful thing has occurred. Books as diverse as Boethius' classic *On the Consolation of Philosophy* (written in 523) and Rabbi Harold S. Kushner's bestseller *When Bad Things Happen to Good People* (1981) have explained that blame—either of self or someone else—dominates human response to the shock that occurs when "normal" has been terminally disrupted. Existential crises are common, as many turn their anger on God. Others imagine themselves justly singled out by God for punishment, experiencing the kind of "moral impostor syndrome" that Molly did—the sense that somehow they've managed to fool God about their worthiness all along, but he's finally decided to lower the long-deserved hammer.[7]

None of this, obviously, is any good for the person's state of mind, nor does it offer any promise of illuminating a constructive way forward. Yet struggling to trace "why" is a natural human tendency. Recently researchers in evolutionary biology have attempted to account for such addiction to causal logic, arguing that human beings' compulsion to understand why things happen goes all the way back to our earliest African savannah days. Early humanoids who recognized patterns in landscape and animal activity, they hypothesize, were better able to hunt game and avoid predators. Having survived to adulthood, such people were more likely to reproduce and pass these pattern-recognition talents along.

Contemporary research in brain chemistry and neurology also supports the hypothesis that members of our species are hard-wired at the physiological, chemical level to be causal logic-driven creatures. Investigating how different parts of the brain receive, process, and store new bits of information from the senses, they've discovered that this organ reflexively attempts to fit fresh data into preexisting categories. Only if we can't make the new information fit do our brains consider adjusting the schema. This process, called "sensemaking," has become an important area of scientific study.[8]

It's undeniably true that this schema-driven way of approaching the world is still useful. The predictive "rules" offered by such internalized patterns can still save lives. (Ever had a hunch that you needed to get out of a place, *now?*) They ease human relationships. (If I do *x* in this interaction with this person, *y* is likely to occur. When my sister says *a*, she really means *b*.) They help us learn and integrate new information. They underlie our basic problem-solving ability, allowing us to move more and more effectively and confidently around the world as the predictive capacity in our brains becomes more accurate, thanks to the constant arrival of new information.

It's only natural, then, for people to panic when something happens that not only requires the tweaking of a schema but blows it to smithereens. In the absence of a pattern's comfortable security, all those ancient terrors come flooding back: *How can I know how to act, stay safe, take any volitional control of circumstances? I've apparently been fooling myself all along about the logic of this world; I can't trust anything now. How can I possibly go forward?* To make matters worse, those who have lost something that was a foundational component of their identity—a mate, a child, a self-defining job, a state of flourishing health, trust in God's ever-dependable protection of them—feel stripped of the assumptions that defined them to themselves.

Consolation minister Beth L. Hewett has used the term "liminal space" for this sense of being helplessly adrift, defining it as the period after loss when a mourner has been forced to admit that the old way of life is gone but cannot yet conceptualize the shape a new one might take. "In grief," she writes, "people cross a threshold from their old lives into the new. Betwixt and between, they reside for a while in a middle space of great mystery" where "existing . . . can be uncomfortable or even frightening." On this threshold they might even suspect they're going insane; they feel "psychically and physically" disoriented as their sense of control and safety has been shattered.[9]

No wonder, then, that our initial response to a life-changing everyday annunciation that comes by way of loss or tragedy is to quake, resist, even flee. In fact, the history of the church confirms that some of the holiest people who ever lived have attempted to resist when their worlds changed.

Consider, for example, Pope Gregory I—a saint who is not called "great" for nothing, having reformed church liturgy, composed and influenced church music, combatted heresy, sent missionaries to England, and authored a wealth of influential letters and treatises.

As a young man from a wealthy family, Gregory served in public office, but after his father died, Gregory sold his worldly goods, founded a monastery, and retired there, having long wished for a life of prayer devoted utterly to God. Recognizing talent when they saw it, however, authorities summoned the administratively talented, highly ethical Gregory back into the world to fill the positions of Deacon of Rome and Ambassador to Byzantium. When these appointments ended Gregory returned gratefully to his monastery.

But then, to his horror, he was summoned again, for he'd been elected pope. In contrast to so many powerful men in the medieval and Renaissance periods who schemed, bribed, even murdered to gain that office, Gregory protested and attempted firmly to decline—to no avail, for the hierarchy insisted that he and he alone must direct the church, and being an obedient man as well as a gifted and faithful one, Gregory eventually relented.

Still, reconciling himself to the "schema" of ultimate ecclesiastical rank and power apparently proved difficult for this saint long after his coronation. In one of Gregory's first treatises as pope, in fact, he frankly informs readers that he feels he's been "forced" against his deep inclination to take on ecclesiastical office, "plunged on a sudden into a sea" of worldly confusions and duties which he did not desire in the least. "That office which withdrew me from the monastery had with the point of its employments stabbed me to death as to my former tranquility of life," Gregory recalls. Biographies of this reluctant pope have documented Gregory's persistent psychic and physical discomfort throughout his papacy, signaled by anxiety-sparked gastritis and colitis. There are many ways the body continues to manifest an echo of ongoing reluctance, it seems, even when a servant of God is disciplining himself to fulfill his calling in the most exemplary way possible.[10]

Reluctance also features so commonly in Bible stories about the callings of prophets that scholars who analyze such narratives consider expressions of reluctance (such as questions and objections) to be part of the "grammar" of the genre. (Food for thought: Elizabeth Johnson places Mary's annunciation in this family of stories.[11])

Examples of this "grammar of reluctance" are easy to find once you start looking for them. No less a God-ordained leader than Moses himself protests, "Who am I that I should go to Pharoah and lead the Israelites out of Egypt?" (Exod 3:11). And he continues protesting even after God guarantees support and offers miracles as convincing proof of Moses' status as a divine representative. He's "slow of speech" (Exod 4:10), Moses argues in one of these later appeals—a popular dodge also proffered by Jeremiah, who voices the additional objection that he's "too young" (Jer 1:6).

The most famous biblical would-be shirker, of course, is Jonah, the details of whose flight make the resistance of Lotto's Mary seem minor. As every Sunday school child knows, Jonah is ordered by God to go and preach against the wickedness of Nineveh. What you might not know is that Nineveh, the Assyrian capital, is in modern-day Iraq, a journey to the northeast of about 550 miles overland from where Jonah lives. When a terrified Jonah flees, he goes in exactly the *opposite* direction, boarding a ship headed to Tarshish, which is 2,500 miles due west across the entire Mediterranean in present-day Spain. It's as if Jonah believes that by this strategy he might disappear from God's GPS. God, of course, is not fooled, and a tempest arises. The sailors throw Jonah overboard, and a "great fish" swallows him. Three days and nights later, Jonah has finally had enough of the dark, dank fish's belly and prays in repentance for his disobedience. Abruptly he's delivered, free to go about God's business as originally requested.

It can take a lot, it seems, to get some people on board.

Futile Resistance

What a weird and striking tale Jonah's is, so full of wonder, terror, archetypal images and themes, almost comically exaggerated in its message: *You can't escape God.* So ancient and foreign and hard to get one's head around![12]

Yet I'm going to confess that of all the tales I've ever heard of futile human attempts to resist a difficult change and even escape God, this is the one that has always seemed subjectively closest to the bone in approximating how my own experience of early widowhood felt.

It's absurd, obviously, to talk about someone "resisting" widowhood. Your spouse dies—an absolute, undebatable thing—and there you are. Yet you can nevertheless refuse emotionally and psychologically even to consider reconciling yourself to the loss, spinning yourself ever more deeply into what psychiatric literature terms "complicated grief," a self-perpetuating loop of anguish fed by guilt and assorted personality issues, convincing yourself that the "whale's belly" of depression is just where you deserve to be for the foreseeable future.

And that's exactly what I did, figuratively running in the opposite direction as hard as I could, hands flapping in the air, mouth forming "no, no, NO!" at the merest suggestion that healing might (or should) be possible.

I hadn't had much practice, you see, in saying "yes" when I didn't want to, or even in accepting "no." Certainly my years on earth had included the usual disappointments and adjustments, the typical sorrows and losses and vows to do better. But all the really important things, the things I most thanked God for providing for me, had fallen into place—a wonderful education, a university career I loved, and my marriage to a kindred spirit I deeply love and who loved me.

In consequence, without really meaning to, I'd become a woman who felt herself to be living a charmed life. I'd even slipped into half-believing that it was largely me who had engineered all those good things, that I was acting as "the master of my fate . . . the captain of my soul," as the self-centered voice in William Ernest Henley's "Invictus," that overblown classic of popular Victorian poetry, proclaims. I was proud of my energy, my ability to make and execute campaigns for this or that. And plans there were, for I believed in those days that everybody needed a clear map of what their futures should hold. "My little guided missile," Ford called me with affectionate amusement, which should have been a clue.

I know, it's paradoxical that, after converting to Catholicism at age 35, I "thanked God" for the things I'd been so proud of achieving under my own power, but I did. And I meant that gratitude, too . . . though in some terminally confused way I'd simultaneously taught myself to believe that while God's grace had charted this happy course, mine were the hands that had managed all those practical details relative to the steering.

Of course, taking the credit also meant taking the blame. When the cancer diagnosis came, when the disease resisted all efforts at cure, and when my husband died, I blamed myself. Stubbornly ignoring the fact that Ford's father and grandfather had also died of prostate cancer in the same decade of their lives, I rehashed our quarrels, our diet, our alcohol consumption, our sex life—all factors said to influence the development of that disease. Why hadn't I taken more care? I fancied that I could still have saved Ford even when the doctors abandoned hope—that I'd missed some obvious miracle cure, that I should have managed his nutrition or rest better, that my own stress had fueled anxiety in him which hormonally accelerated the cancer.

Reprising the theology of Job's comforters, I convinced myself that God was punishing me for the vainglory of imagining that I was particularly good, particularly beloved by the Mystery that created me, or for any number of sins—for arrogance, self-absorption, pride, gossip, carelessness in religious observance. Perhaps God had been laughing at me all the time that I'd been so happy. Perhaps the whole construct of my so-comfortable "normal" had been a cruel tease, like that recounted in Puritan preacher Jonathan Edward's sermon, "Sinners in the Hands of an Angry God," with me in the role of the loathsome, clueless spider suspended over the pit. What conceivable right did I have to imagine that I might be allowed ever to "move on" into a satisfying new life?

There's good guilt, of course, as John J. Boucher wrote in an insightful *Catholic Digest* article, healthy guilt that serves "as an invitation to stop, to review our lives, and to change . . . and be converted through the mercy of the Holy Spirit."[13] But the guilt I felt in early widowhood was the corrosive sort, the variety that Boucher terms "unreasonable, beyond our control, and . . . self-centered," the kind that divides us from God, others, and our best selves.

Can you say "dank"? Can you say "dark"?

More to the point, in my case, can you say "self-destructive"? Believing I deserved punishment, I turned my own hands and heart to that effort, though I soon discovered myself to be a physical coward when it came to outright self-destruction. Nevertheless, suicide seemed a concept with somewhat liquid boundaries, and for a while there was a lot of feinting at that ultimate "no." Not previously an accident-prone person, within the first year of bereavement my "careless" mishaps led to injuries which a foot or two of difference would have made much worse. I cracked two ribs; I sprained my ankle; I pulled my neck; I clenched my hip muscles and gave myself back pain and sciatica. In an episode that at least led to some comic relief, I broke a finger so badly that it had to be splinted for months . . . and fittingly, it was a middle finger, making obvious my attitude toward just about everything that terrible first summer of widowhood. I symbolically obliterated myself, too, in despair-induced muddled states of mind, repeatedly throwing my drivers' license and/or checkbook and/or car keys in the trash without realizing it, until I missed them in the morning. I indulged in appallingly risky behaviors, driving recklessly on mountain roads, drinking myself silly while taking sleeping pills, walking alone in the dark in unfamiliar towns when I traveled for work. I courted social suicide, too, picking fights with friends, isolating myself by saying I had other plans when I didn't.

"God doesn't give you more than you can handle," the platitude goes. But for a while there, I'd definitely taken myself right up to that limit, and maybe beyond.

Top-Down Grace

The proverbial advice for someone in such a state, of course, is to do what Jonah did: discard your pride, say you're sorry for whatever it is you've done, and pray for help. If such a person believes that she's finally been "outed" as irredeemably sinful and worthless, however, and moreover doesn't believe that there's anything left to live for, such prayer will not come naturally to her lips. And so I extended for several years that attempt at flight.

Until—in what I've come to believe was an expression of breath-taking grace—God apparently got so tired of waiting for me to seek divine wisdom that divine mercy took the initiative, coaxing me out of that slough of despondency into which I'd so perversely run. How sneaky God was. So subtle, so utterly familiar with my nature, dangling in front of me the one reason to go on living that my creator knew I couldn't resist: the soul-deep pleasure any born teacher feels in mentoring students who are struggling to find their way.

The first time a troubled student dropped by my office seeking a listening ear and sympathetic counseling seemed happenstance, as did the second. But soon the flow formed a pattern that was impossible to ignore. I'd never been the sort of teacher to whom students came to cry when everything went to pieces in their lives (looking back, it was no wonder, for who in such straits would dream of empathy from somebody who so obviously prided herself on having everything together?). But now lost ones began to regularly drop by without appointments; they turned paper conference sessions into confessionals; they ambushed me after class to request "just a few minutes" of my time.

Who would ever have guessed that so much human misery walked the halls of the liberal arts building? Not me. "I had to give him up," a suicidal young poet wept of her infant, yielded from her arms to an adoptive family to save him from the haze of abuse and excess that marked her relationship with the child's father. "My parents have sacrificed everything to get me here," a first-generation immigrant—who wasn't even in one of my classes but had been referred by someone who was—cried as she described rejection from the pre-professional program that had been a source of family pride. "He was so much better than me," a young man mumbled, tears running down his face, as he recounted the car accident that killed his best friend. "It was my fault. I should have been the one to die."

How had they known I would be accepting, understanding? The first time I taught *The Scarlet Letter* after being thrust into this mother-confessor sideline, I suddenly fancied I knew the answer. Just like Hawthorne's fallen heroine Hester Prynne, I'd apparently acquired some kind of mark to distinguish me from all those happy, "normal" people who'd been allowed blissfully unruffled, conventional lives—not a letter sown onto my clothing, but an invisible emanation that was pulsing, beckoning, identifying me as a displaced person, too.

To my great surprise, I found myself easy in their presence, for these distraught people no longer made me nervous, as they once would have. Now it was instinctive to listen with patience, letting those sisters and brothers of tragedy spill their sorrow without feeling any anxious, reflexive compulsion to fix the unfixable as quickly as possible. I heard admissions of guilt—guilt that was a familiar mixture of potentially constructive insight and utterly dysfunctional self-blame. I let people cry. I nodded and accepted. I hugged when that was invited, though I'd *never* been the sort of person who hugged strangers. I joined in brainstorming about what their now-uncertain futures might look like, hearing myself counsel, *Take your time. Don't necessarily try to recreate the past. What are some things you might do now?* If the person in the other chair was so far underwater that no viable next act came to mind, I asked about the dreams she'd had for herself as a child and teenager. And I sometimes confessed my own struggles in the foggy world of liminality, admitting kinship. For who was I, after all, to pretend that I was somehow set apart from all this human woe, that I had all the answers?

Walking through gathering dusk to my car one autumn afternoon, I found myself replaying the day's last conversation, the third or fourth with a forty-something woman whose husband had recently filed for divorce. *She's got to get out of that self-flagellation stage,* I thought. *This whole loop is becoming incredibly self-destructive. A loving God wouldn't want to see any soul forever stuck in such anguish, no matter what they've done.*

Abruptly, *finally,* my own kind words found their way back to me, there in the middle of that empty parking lot.

Surrendering . . . And Talking Back

In one of singer-songwriter-poet Joni Mitchell's songs, a man speaks of having "sacrificed [his] blues" in the search for love[14]—a profound insight, it's always seemed to me, and one vividly relevant for those who have struggled with depression. Misery can become a such a familiar companion that it constitutes a homey comfort zone, one whose landscape, though uncomfortable, is at least understood. Choosing to move beyond such a trough can feel very risky indeed, as if you're going to goose the gods who justly imposed it, as if you're going to lose a fundamental part of yourself.

On the afternoon I've just described, however, thanks to a loving God who apparently retained at least enough faith in me to employ me in these modest works of mercy (and also thanks to the memory of Fra Angelico's Mary, and to simply being tired of being miserable), I finally agreed to try.

In its early days that contract was decidedly short-term, a series of "that was just for today" agreements. On the worst days, the ones when fight-or-flight adrenaline surged through my system to wake me hours before dawn, I still struggled mightily with those blues and temptations, and sometimes I slipped back downward.

In this new phase of trying, however, when such things happened, I willed myself to take the advice I'd given to others. I dutifully distracted myself with changes of scenery, reading an interesting new book, coffee with a friend, a recorded symphony, a challenging knitting pattern. I calmed my pounding heart with meditation, slowing my respiration with the Ayurvedic color breathing technique Ford had employed during his illness. I made lists of simple blessings each evening and set intentions for the day each morning. Guess what? Those strategies worked. Something was happening in my heart, my soul, my metabolism. Echoing Sr. Bernadette's phrase, I came to think of the process as "being seduced back to life."

But *why* was I being seduced? All I'd wanted was to die and join Ford, and I still craved that deeply. But apparently this God, who appeared to be talking to me again—and who presumably felt some mercy toward me—had some reason to keep me hanging on. Perhaps I just wasn't getting it. Maybe there was an expectation on God's part about a particular service, or a critical mass of good works, that I needed to accomplish before I'd be allowed to have my heart's desire.

I'm not saying I literally believed such things, but there seemed no harm in trying out the "good works" theory. And looking back it's hard to imagine an idea that would have served me better at the time. All remaining traces of lassitude disappeared as I supplemented the informal counseling I was already doing with bushels of good works. Make calls and help fill out complicated paperwork for a young woman in need of a special program? Check. Provide extra help to a student struggling with the next assignment for my class? Check. Write an essay about mourning that might ease somebody else's path? Organize and direct a public humanities grant for teachers who needed support and validation? Offer friendly greetings and compliments to everyone I met who appeared downcast? Help the lady with the cane bring her trashcan in from the curb? Drop by the laundromat just to leave a $10 bill in one of the change slots? Let go of that last bit of anger toward God, get back on the lector and eucharistic minister schedules, then join the music ministry? Check, check, and check.

I'm serious—I did all these things and more, wryly assuring myself that each one might be that elusive balance tipper. As they piled up, though, I realized that such good works were becoming happy ends in themselves, that I was rising each day with eagerness to see what possibilities for service the day might hold. A very good and tricky Shepherd, indeed, appeared to be nudging me toward a reason to believe, perhaps even a reason to live.

Then one winter night I nudged back.

I've forgotten exactly what good works I'd completed that day. What I do remember is that as I offered up whatever they were, the sense dawned that for a while now I'd been giving more than I was getting. If God was indeed keeping a ledger, heavenly accounting practices verged on usurious.

Neither do I recall deciding to go out on the deck in the role of righteously indignant petitioner, but suddenly there I was, under the dark winter sky. Luckily houses are widely spaced in my mountain neighborhood, for before I knew it, I was shaking my fist at the stars, speaking bluntly to God like an irritated friend who has a right to do so, like some wits-end Old Testament prophet, like some sheet-draped, flowing-haired character in a 1950s biblical epic film. "God damn it, God!" The words just popped out as I spread my hands in the classic palms-up gesture of frustration. "Isn't that sufficient? Can't you beam me up now?"

Abruptly, I was laughing. There was no sense fighting; God's will would be done, and I'd better get used to that if I was "doomed" to go on living.

"Whatever," I said aloud that night, taking a deep breath and ostentatiously bowing, offering an undignified version of "Let it be done to me" with not bad humor, relaxing the protective hug my arms had figuratively provided for so long, and stretching them open, toward the sky. "At your service, Sir," I heard myself say.

✦ ✦ ✦

When you're struggling for balance after everything's changed, it can feel like you're doomed forever "to go [on], like iron or rock, day after day, as [God] pleases and how he pleases," as St. Elizabeth Ann Seton remarked when her family members and religious sisters died in close succession during an epidemic. Yet there's wonderful possibility offered, too, for all—like Seton, like Lotto's Mary, even like the self-sabotaging case I once was.

It's undeniably difficult—even terrifying, given how it goes against all the ways our bodies have taught themselves to make sense—to take a vulnerable "leap of free cooperation" into an uncertain, God-determined future, a future we cannot know or predict.[15]

What kind of God could let this happen to me? Who will I be without the one I love? How can I go forward now that I can't imagine any "rest of the story" that I want to embrace? How can this be?

These are good and natural questions, no doubt about it . . . archetypal questions in the human repertoire. But let me suggest that sooner or later, the time must come when an infinitely more constructive question—the one that I was finally, patiently brought to ask—can become our response to our most painful annunciations:

So, what now?

Guido Reni, *The Annunciation*, 1631–32.

Chapter Three

Annunciations that Change Everything, Part Two

Faithful Discernment as a Way Forward

The young woman looks wonderfully calm as the incarnating light descends, appearing to cherish that experience in her heart and consider it with curiosity and wonder in her mind. There is no sign of shrinking in her expression or posture despite the potential consequences of the "yes" she's just said, among them the fact that as an engaged girl who has not yet lived with her husband, a pregnancy makes her liable to stoning for adultery. Yet, she's surrendering to God's will so trustingly.

Such composure is even more remarkable given that she kneels in the midst of unabashedly staring heavenly beings, for she has lived as a modest peasant girl, not important enough to merit the attention of such great ones. The angel Gabriel stands just a few feet away, staring with a rapt, fixed gaze. An angel in the heavens points at her as one might point at a celebrity glimpsed in the street, directing focus so the other heavenly beings don't miss her. And that beam of light shining down on her signals that the greatest one of all, God the Father, is also giving her undivided attention.

Yet the young woman shows no pride at such distinction. Instead, she rests in a posture that Renaissance Annunciation art cognoscenti would have recognized as signifying *humiliatio* (submission). The northern Italian painter Guido Reni has depicted Mary in this work with lowered head and eyes; she rests on her knees, her hands joined in a prayer of reverence and trust.

Nevertheless, there's a paradox here, for that stream of light reminds attentive viewers that even as Mary bows her head in *humiliatio*, she's simultaneously engaged in *meritatio* (meritorious response), the active component of responding to that heavenly invitation. She's voluntarily conceiving Jesus in her womb, committing of her own free will to whatever her part in the divine plan might be. The nuances of her posture reinforce the impression of active confidence, for she holds her body upright in calm dignity. Her reflective face registers that a rich inner life is already working away at this mystery—that she's no mere passive receptacle but a woman who might be proclaiming with the psalmist, "I will ponder your precepts and consider your paths. . . . Open my eyes to see clearly the wonders of your law" (Ps 119:15, 18).

In this elegant depiction of the annunciation, Mary is at once obedient and confident, simultaneously instrument and agent—an aspirational model, as Christian faith has long held, of how believers should respond when God says, *Trust me.*

Yet it's important to emphasize that word "aspirational," given this painting's circumstances of production, since neither the man who created that image (notorious for his ego and self-promotion), nor the woman for whom it was created (Marie de Medici, the French regent queen so jealous of power, so conniving that her own son twice banished her from court for her intrigues) was ever famous for saying "Let it be."[1]

Nevertheless, the fact that Reni conceived and executed this concept so evocatively and Marie de Medici admired it so much that she displayed it prominently in her grandest palace does suggest something encouraging if you're struggling to cope with a difficult everyday annunciation of your own. It implies that pretty much any Christian can appreciate the glory of the kind of faith this Annunciation depicts, a faith that balances the humility of human surrender with the dignity of human agency.

And if you can dream it, as they say . . .

Yearning for Safety and Certainty

"O clemens, O pia," my voice rises in harmony with my fellow musicians' at this climax of the ravishingly beautiful Marian hymn "Salve Regina." My whole body has become an instrument, words and vibrations of tone resonating through tissue and muscle, brain and heart. Everybody in the congregation is singing, some with eyes closed to better focus on the yearning supplication. Meditating on Mary's grace has transformed an ordinary 8:00 a.m. Sunday Mass into a peak spiritual experience where longing, gratitude, and a sense of common humanity bind us together.

Magical though it might feel, there's nothing surprising in such a communal outpouring, really, for the world offers so much to trouble us, so many reasons to yearn toward Mary as a merciful, loving, heavenly intercessor. She's uniquely qualified to understand our pain, since her own "yes" was not a guarantee of an easy life but an agreement to be faithful through what must have been confusing challenges, from annunciation to empty tomb and beyond. *Even Mary,* we might all say, taking comfort in this loving mentor who, while holding a uniquely privileged position in heaven, "gets" our confusion and anguish over life's seemingly inexplicable turnings.

Of course, we're also *not* like her in a pivotal way. She was born without sin; we're full of it. Faced with our own annunciations large or even small, we rarely achieve anything like Mary's willingness to rest in uncertainty, to trust God to work in us. How many sad strategies our fears and insecurities prompt—all tacit ways of proclaiming, "I'd prefer not to, God."

I spoke in the previous chapter about my own depression, situational alcoholism, and suicidal thoughts. I've watched acquaintances turn to enervating painkillers and other drugs that interfere with the process of thinking about how they might move forward in constructive *meritatio*, Renaissance art theory's term for Mary's obedience bodied forth in action. I've seen others attempt to end-run the challenge of remaining open to God's will by attempting to recreate a "new normal" that looks as much like the "old normal" as possible. Among the most memorable was a man in his eighties who was a member of the grief group I attended the autumn after Ford's death. On the group's first night Hiram couldn't even say his wife's name aloud, breaking down into heaving sobs and tears. During our meetings in the following weeks, he remained silent, sitting with lowered eyes, listening to the rest of us grapple with grief and anger, firmly shaking his head when invited to share. So when this bereft man stopped attending by the sixth week we naturally worried . . . until at our final session a group member shared a clipping from the local newspaper's wedding page which pictured Hiram, beaming, his arm draped around the shoulders of a new bride who was young enough to be his daughter (a woman whose smile was *much* more tenuous).

To allow Hiram a bit of slack, they both belonged to a faith tradition that strongly believes adults ought to come in couples, that structures its religious observances and church-sponsored social life around marital roles, and that is locally rumored to match up widowers and widows expeditiously so that "man should not be alone." Nevertheless, although of course I hope that devastated older man and that uncertain younger woman are having a very happy life together, it seems to me that such a rush back to the safe harbor of marriage might not, under the circumstances, have been the best idea in the world.

Such cynicism aside, I "totally get" (as my students would say) how daunting it is to still the natural urge to be settled, the panic we human beings feel when we sense ourselves to be "outside" the normal way that we think everybody is supposed to live. And there are plenty of people who, after adequate time, prayer, counseling, or spiritual advising come to the true and noble conclusion that marriage is where they're supposed to be. An especially happy example exists in our parish, in fact, featuring an elderly woman who for forty years built an amazing, loving marriage in which she and her husband supported not just their own extensive family, but also many "dear strays," as she likes to say, folding them into community with hospitality and love. After his death she took a while to heal and recenter herself, drawing on the care of loved ones, the solace and guidance of prayer and reflection, as well as experience out in the community trying on various kinds of volunteer service. About a year later she reaffirmed her primary calling toward marriage by wedding her late husband's best friend, a man the couple had loved like a brother, a single man with no family who had spent much time with them. Knowing each other well and united in faith, both seeking companionship and comfort and dedicated to extending fellowship to others, they've built a wonderful, useful, loving new life together.

I acknowledge, too, that I was very lucky in that the defining vocation of my occupational career remained after my husband's death. Nevertheless, my marital vocation, the calling that told me who I was socially and relationally, had imploded, and I'll admit that for a while after being widowed I too daydreamed that my personal future might involve remarriage. But rationally I knew that choice to be folly given what an emotional/physical/spiritual mess I was, and how deeply in love I still was with my husband.

Of course, this did not deter well-intentioned friends from recommending books and movies about widows who "moved on." In this genre marrying again is pretty much universally recommended as the perfect answer to the question, "How might my life have meaning again?" Second choice is moving to some beautiful other country where a widow can "find herself" during extended leisure, not an option in my case. Living for your kids comes in a distant—though righteous—third. But I had no kids, so ditto.

I began to dread the future, knowing that even the occupation cocoon wasn't a viable long-term solution for that "Who am I now?" question since retirement loomed just a decade ahead. Sure, I'd keep writing; no doubt about that. But once I retired from the university (as I had no doubt I'd welcome doing—no hanging around for me), there would be no daily human contact, none of the constant reinforcement of making a difference for somebody that was then sustaining me. A woman couldn't sit in her house alone and write all day, every day, without potentially endangering her mental health—at least I couldn't, with my lifelong tendency to depression. What in the world was I going to do with myself?

One summer evening in the grip of what my husband would have called "a big case of the now-whats," I found myself reminiscing with envy and nostalgia about my undergraduate years, when my friends and I were attempting to understand what our places in the world might be. How reassuring it was when constant opportunities for forming new friendships and dating made "finding yourself" seem normal rather than like a lonely, weirdly out-of-season burden.

Maybe the time for new starts and new dreams had in fact passed. Perhaps the restless unease and fruitless yearning I felt indicated that it was absurd even to think about getting comfortable with a "new me." Nevertheless, I needed to think of *something*.

But as it turns out, what I needed wasn't clearer reasoning, career counseling, more effective problem-solving strategies, or the fortitude to suck it up and get comfortable with what seemed destined to be some anticlimactic, lame-duck years ahead. What I needed was a completely different paradigm—the spiritual paradigm of Guido Reni's Mary—in which everything wasn't up to me, though I was certainly expected to do my part.

Necessary Wandering

If you're familiar with the literature of spiritual seeking, you may be shaking your head and smiling at this point, understanding that the "wilderness" of late middle age, in which I felt myself unmoored and wandering, has been very well-populated over the ages—and well-mapped, for psychologists and spiritual teachers from many traditions have described such between-time and the existential discomfort it involves.

Oddly enough for a Catholic, it was the Hindu take on aging and spirituality that first prompted me toward the conclusion that such discontent, while admittedly uncomfortable, is a natural and necessary phase of growth for anyone who aspires to later years rich in a sense of new vocation, in maturing faith.

This way of thinking was opened to me in the spring following that memorable winter night out on the deck, at an actual ashram on a warm island in another country—a setting whose exoticism made it even more memorable (and credible) than it would otherwise have been. I'd chosen that destination for spring break on a whim because A) all the beloved places where Ford and I had spent our spring breaks were still too badly haunted; B) my back was still killing me and a class at our community rec center had suggested that yoga could at least somewhat mitigate that; and C) I'd heard that the spiritual aspects of yoga could "help a person find peace," and peace was definitely something I needed.

While that March week was not terribly effective for my back (so challenging was even the beginner yoga class that the localized ache was quickly subsumed into general pain), it did introduce me to a peace-inducing practice I've treasured ever since, the discipline of musical sacred chant. Called "Kirtan" in the Hindu tradition, it involves recitation of the names that culture gives to the divine force. This gentle, swirling repetition remarkably calmed my mind and body from the first moment I walked into the funky little open-air pavilion where it was being sung. It quickly earned its place in my arsenal of "techniques for distracting and calming Susan," and after I returned home, it also (ironically) led me right back into my own faith (very funny, God) by prompting me to explore the Christian tradition of Gregorian chant, a practice that to this day is among the mainstays of my Catholic spiritual life.

But as I've already mentioned, the real game changer of the week was an introduction to the Hindu approach to aging. Having signed up for an afternoon session on "Asrama" without knowing what that meant (I liked the sound of the word, and most crucially it was billed as a lecture, not another agonizing physical class!), I discovered much to ponder. "Asrama," as I learned that day, indicates the four successive seasons into which Hindus divide a properly conducted life, all of which are necessary for spiritual advancement. First comes the student phase (Brahmacharya), then the householder period (Grihastha), when marriage, productivity, and social convention dominate people's concerns. The third phase (Vanaprastha) involves withdrawing in elder years from the mundane concerns of Grihastha in order to pursue spiritual awareness (Vanaprastha is also called the "forest walker" stage, a phrase that gave me chills, for the only activity that reliably afforded me any real contentment in that period was solitary wandering in my backyard mountains). The final phase is Sannyasa, or ascetic, where an aged person's whole focus becomes preparation for death and rebirth.[2]

How helpful this framework proved for me at exactly that moment! How it sustained me with assurance that my unmoored condition was both proper and desirable for a person of my age . . . especially when, returning home at week's end, I reentered a world dominated by people who acted as if any existence which wasn't preoccupied with matters of job, family, shopping, sports, keeping up the house, socializing, etc., was odd. I'll confess that for some time after that visit to the ashram, as a self-proclaimed, proud Vanaprastha I derived considerable comfort from sneering internally at such "clueless householders." The impulse was petty, yes (and a misrepresentation of the Hindu tradition), but this attitude provided *exactly* the reinforcement I needed to help me own that I was on an archetypal, perfectly appropriate developmental schedule.

What a refreshing idea—that later years were supposed to be dignified by the work of seeking existential truth. And that, at some point, in order to become spiritually whole, we *have* to lose the very normalcy whose absence I'd been lamenting.

Christian Perspectives

I should have already considered such ideas, of course, for in the Christian tradition old age with its losses has also been understood as an especially auspicious time for spiritual development. How did I miss all those Scripture verses, all those stories of saints and ancient ones who devoted themselves ever more deeply to the work of faith as they aged?

But later is better than never, and eventually—thanks initially to the 2011 publication of Richard Rohr's *Falling Upward: A Spirituality for the Two Halves of Life*—I discovered the very unsecret truth that the Catholic faith also holds that faith and identity ought to evolve through all of life's seasons.

Rohr's argument, in a nutshell, is that later years are not merely "a very acceptable time" (2 Cor 6:2) to focus on seeking a deeper relationship with God, but a uniquely proper time. As Rohr explains it, young adults necessarily have a lot of other things to think about during their years of "ego structuring"—defining who they are, establishing their niches in society, gaining security. Through this process young people create "containers" for their identities, secure sets of assumptions that allow them to operate with confidence in what might seem to be a chaotic, non-user-friendly world.

Nevertheless, sooner or later, Rohr assures his readers, "if you are on any classic 'spiritual schedule,' some event, person, death, idea, or relationship will enter your life that you cannot deal with using your present skill set, your acquired knowledge, or your strong willpower." Though such imperatives can feel like catastrophes, Rohr explains that they function as goads to evolution. Without them we can become stuck in a simplistic set of habits and beliefs, dangerously convinced of our individual ego's power, never reaching toward a more mature understanding of the self that God wants us to be.[3]

"Necessary suffering," the writer Gerald W. Hughes has termed such growing pains. "Our God is a God of surprise," he writes (employing the theologian Karl Rahner's term), a Father "who, in the darkness and the tears of things, breaks down our false images and securities. This in-breaking can feel like disintegration, but it is the disintegration of an ear of wheat . . . if it does not die to begin new life, it shrinks away on its own."[4]

Thomas Merton, whose classic book *New Seeds of Contemplation* (1961) was an important influence on Rohr, asserts forcefully that to claim full dignity as a child of God one *must* cast off the secure, self-serving conventional roles of what *New Seeds* pejoratively terms the "false self" (shades of my militantly anti-householder phase!). According to Merton, all who desire to grow close to God have no choice but to dare to undertake, through prayer and contemplation, "the problem of finding out who I am and of discovering my true self."

Fortunately for us, Merton assures his readers, we're not alone in this daunting quest; we can trust that an all-loving God will prove tireless in helping us discover our holy potential. Indeed, we can feel sure that even the faintest prompting to plumb the true self is a clear indication that God is *already* working in us. "It is not we who choose to awaken ourselves," he writes, "but God who chooses in love to awaken us" so that we can "make the choices that deliver us from our routine self and open . . . the door of a new being, a new reality."

We should also draw confidence, Merton writes, from knowing that God has already invested our natures with the unique traits and talents necessary for the role we need to fill. Even seemingly unfortunate or quirky tendencies can prove to be exactly what's needed for our unique vocations to play out. Every experience— events, people encountered, missteps, successes, "chances" which at the time appeared very minor—can function as "seed[s] planted in [our] liberty . . . by God's will . . . the seeds of [our] own identity . . . [our] own sanctity."[5]

How joyfully encouraging this perspective is, as it emphasizes God's enduring faith in us, God's commitment to helping us do the work necessary to bloom into the creatures we've been created to be. Indeed, this teaching is so different from the extremes of "fire and brimstone" preaching that it might seem almost too good to be true. Yet so many confirming examples exist: how St. John Vianney's understanding of those who struggle, inspired by having been a very poor student, helped make him a peerless confessor; or how a "chance" encounter with St. Teresa of Avila's autobiography became the seed that set the agnostic Edith Stein on the path to becoming a religious sister, one whose academic interest in empathy emerged into a selfless love of others so deep that later, Stein voluntarily accompanied others to a Nazi death camp, dedicating herself to comforting women and babies before her own murder.

Seeking Direction

It's one thing, of course, *theoretically* to affirm the desirability of sloughing off a "false self" and opening ourselves to divine guidance, and quite another to imagine exactly *how* we might go about achieving that magnificent mixture of surrender and creative agency that Reni's Mary models. What exactly might "kneeling" or "turning to God" look like for us in the twenty-first century? How much "bowing of the head" is appropriate, and at what point does submissive waiting become unfruitful passivity? What features of our past are trying to get our attention? How can we discover the unique, creative, generative capacities God has placed in us and employ them rightly, as Mary did?

If such questions currently resonate with you, an ideal place to turn is the age-old practice of reverent investigation that modern spiritual advising calls "discernment"—a discipline whose examples in Scripture include Jesus' time of fasting in the wilderness and Mary's "pondering" (Luke 2:19, 51). And among the best guides to undertaking it, I believe, is the renowned spiritual director and author Henri Nouwen. A brilliant man trained in psychology and theology, Nouwen worked for years as a university professor at Notre Dame, Harvard, and Yale divinity schools; he became an internationally sought speaker, a famous spiritual director, and a bestselling writer. Yet, as his mental health deteriorated, Nouwen came to understand that insecurity about being lovable or good enough had made him dangerously addicted to praise and fame. After struggling for years to discard what he considered this "false self" and find his true calling, Nouwen finally discovered deep fulfillment and personal peace in his last years as a chaplain at a residential L'Arche community for people with mental disabilities, a living situation emphasizing dignity and love.[6]

When Nouwen writes about the challenges of discernment, he's drawing on intimate personal experiences which included severe depression, nervous breakdowns, loneliness, crises of faith, and self-confessed struggles with ego. Candid and humble, he's not afraid to "get in the weeds" by confessing missteps and difficulties as well as describing specific strategies that have characterized his "active waiting on a God who waits for us" to know the divine will. As Nouwen describes discernment, it's not a logical, rational process of decision-making that we control with our intellect. Instead, it's a humble opening that requires us to wait and pay attention—a process that calls for patience, faith, and the willingness to respond at the proper time, a process that depends on accepting that God *will* be salting our world with promptings (Merton's "seeds") that can guide us if we'll only open our eyes and ears and start looking for them.

The essence of Nouwen's counsel is to pay attention to the subtle "signs of daily life" that are nothing other than God reaching into the fabric of reality. The people God puts in our path, things we read or hear regarding faith or current events in our world, dreams, personal experiences, chance encounters and conversations, moments in nature, etc., all hold the potential to awaken us in ways we need to be awakened. Our part of the "dance," as Nouwen describes it, involves cultivating a habit of noticing and responding with focused attention when such things spark an intuitive response, striking us as curious, profound, and interesting. When we realize that our minds and emotions keep coming back to a particular occurrence (or when similar occurrences accumulate), we are to "read" that sign in an effort to "seek to understand what God is trying to say."

Nouwen recommends that such "reading" take the form of setting aside time to ponder such signs in our hearts and minds;

to explore them in conversations with spiritual guides and with compassionate, frank individuals who know us well; and to journal about them. Ask yourself, he suggests, whether what feels like a sign reveals something about the way you're living your life that might be pleasing or disappointing to God, or about a capacity in yourself that you have not yet discovered. Does it awaken you to awareness of another's needs, needs you might help address? Does it remind you of a scriptural passage or an event from the life of someone holy (or not holy)? Does it appear to be leading you toward a constructive response to something in your past? And—humor me as I add one more question I've found very helpful—does it echo or evoke something you've observed or heard or sung at Mass lately?[7]

Prayer is for Nouwen an absolute, obligatory cornerstone of this discernment process, the space in which such pondering should occur. And it's a practice that can take many forms, including but not limited to set prayers (the Lord's Prayer, the rosary, etc.), reading a psalm that resonates with current concerns, offering a personal supplication or complaint, or a spontaneous "cry of the heart" (as St. Thérèse of Lisieux termed prayer). Prayer doesn't even have to involve explicitly "talking to God"—asking for things or advice, laying out feelings in detail—but can be practiced with no words at all, simply by sitting and opening ourselves to God's presence, just "looking at God while he looks at us."[8]

Nouwen cautions that, whatever approach we use to put ourselves in God's presence, we should never expect an immediate answer, for discernment can seem at times protracted, arid, even boring. What's important is to show up, start the conversation, and dedicate ourselves to listening with psychological/spiritual openness. For God, Nouwen insists, is properly understood not as a lofty being who speaks to us only on special occasions, but a loving force that holds conversations in real, continuous time.

That last phrase, "in real, continuous time," deserves emphasis, since some assume that taking an extended retreat is the best or only way truly to explore what God might want of them. While not denying the benefits of retreats, Nouwen emphasizes that the still, small voice of holy wisdom whispers in the midst of mundane routine as well as in silent rooms of hermitages. Indeed, he implies that not only can discernment take place in "normal life," but it properly *should* . . . for it's in that everyday context, after all, that the signs will be most diverse, abundant, and immediately applicable to the contexts in which we move, and where the eventual fruits of discernment will be shared.[9]

Stretching Toward Trust

I've written earlier about the initial "sign of daily life" that I was able to notice in my own everyday environment, that parade of wounded students who sought me out for counsel. What a blessing that phenomenon proved, confirming that I still had a role on earth, turning me toward "yes" and opening my mind to the possibility that something good might be made not just in spite of the loss I'd suffered . . . but perhaps *out of* it, as a sort of homage to my husband and our love.

After the ashram class and the wisdom of those contemporary Christian sages had combined to fertilize my imagination and my soul, I decided it was time to begin paying serious attention, as Nouwen advised, to the seeds God might be planting. What did I have to lose? My antennas went up, my prayer became more frequent and purposeful, my journal full of notes and speculations.

If you smell a whiff of the old "guided missile" here you're right, for a lifelong habit of steering is hard to break, and initially my discernment shaded toward a self-improvement project. So eager was I to feel intuition that I invented it; so excited to get on with this great and noble project that I rushed and forced it. In truth I made a lot of messes as I struggled to achieve basic competence in reading the signs of daily life. Looking back, it's obvious that the misreading and blundering were especially egregious when I wasn't really interested in waiting for God but yielded to an uncomfortable need or fear or weakness and attempted to force a way forward. Tired of feeling like a nobody, I accepted an invitation to join a prestigious nonprofit board of directors . . . but that invitation had obviously not been a "sign," for the fit was all wrong, and before long I ended up awkwardly resigning. Wishing to fill empty hours, I volunteered for new forms of service in the parish and community, only to discover that I lacked the gifts and talents crucial for such work (as honest, preliminary reflection would have indicated). Feeling lonely, longing to be "seen," I grasped at new friendships that proved incompatible and ruptured with hard feelings; I entered into a relationship with a good, loving man that ultimately just didn't work.

Yet over time such fumbling did improve my understanding of how to unclench my hands from the steering wheel, dial down the anxiety, and accept that there were two of us invested in this effort (and that I was the minor party). Sometimes, I eventually accepted, we just have to resign ourselves to kneeling and bowing our heads for a *l-o-n-g* and patient stretch, letting the divine will work in us until we're ready to comprehend. Only then is it appropriate to suggest our own productive spins on whatever it is God has in mind.

In a spiritual sense that initial season of discernment felt every bit as rigorous as the ashram's yoga class . . . and not infrequently left my soul every bit as "sore" from the stretching I was being asked to do. But it was a miniscule price to pay for what has flowed from it—from that time in my life when I first grasped just how patient, persistent, and stunningly creative our Heavenly Father is willing to be in working with anyone who is willing to seek divine guidance.

In good time—time that moved so slowly, it seemed, in some stretches, and so quickly, in firework bursts, in others—I was led to find the direction I'd been longing for. Or *two* life-giving directions, more accurately: a prompting to turn my longtime writing practice more directly to spiritual ends, and a call to embark on a whole new career ministering to others through touch. What a finesser God proved to be as that dual invitation process unfolded, ever so gradually planting the seeds of suggestion, then nudging, then reinforcing with signs aplenty.

The initial "hint" regarding the change in writing direction was delivered way back in 2003, when I'd attempted to force healing by taking an individual retreat at the Benedictine women's monastery where Bernadette lived. Even the compassionate, holy women there couldn't make me all better just a year after Ford's death, of course, but as one counseled me, she did make a suggestion that foreshadowed what would be my first book for a Catholic publisher. During a session when I wondered aloud—again—whether I had let God down or God had let me down, Sr. Martha gently suggested that saints could be good models for those who were wondering how they could ever trust God again. *Just what I need, more flaying*, my mind protested (for my catechetical training on this subject had been thin, and I was mentally conflating saints and martyrs). What my voice said was more polite: that although I revered the saints, it was beyond me to imitate such perfect people.

"Think again," Sr. Martha in essence replied, explaining that in fact these holy men and women had been quirky, interesting, and varied, touched by original sin just like the rest of us. Their distinction lay in *what they did with* that human nature. In fact, she confessed, saints had repeatedly helped her find reconciliation with the divine will when her faith had wavered in response to her mother's cancer, when Vatican II changed convent life, when she'd suffered from clinical depression. "Maybe," I said, being polite. But at that stage I was still unable to focus on much of anything and far from convinced that I really deserved to be healed.

A few years later, however, her advice sprouted up into my consciousness again thanks to one of those graceful "happenstances" so noteworthy in my life during that period—a funny one, in fact, where the joke was on me. Intending to attend services on the feast of All Souls to pray for Ford, I confused the dates and instead walked into an All Saints' Mass. Too embarrassed to leave, I resigned myself to giving up an hour which could have been used for grading papers . . . but was surprised by how the liturgy comforted and inspired me. Referencing St. Augustine, the priest said something that brought Sr. Martha's counsel back to mind.

It was a mistake, he emphasized, to imagine saints as utterly different from us. He explained that those we were celebrating that day were flesh-and-blood humans who hadn't gained their merit through some kind of extraordinary innate characteristics, but via the operation of divine grace. He pointed out that the day's reading from Revelation, "Salvation comes from our God" (7:10), emphasizes that concept, since there was no hope of those saints winning their crowns through their own merits alone. Paradoxically, only by becoming poor in spirit and admitting that we need and long for God's help—as the saints did—can we hope to grow in merit ourselves.

I thought about the implications of that wisdom often in the weeks that followed, acknowledging how it addressed the impatience and self-propulsion into which I was slipping yet again. Finally, as the spring semester started and encouraged thoughts of new beginnings, my mind opened to the possibility that consulting the saints' examples might indeed help address this current spiritual rut.

Here the story gets a bit uncanny, for just two days later, a woman from church who was downsizing sent a group email offering for sale her four-volume hardbound edition of Alban Butler's nineteenth-century *Lives of the Saints*.[10] Fate is hard to resist when it comes at a bargain price, and by the following afternoon, that venerable compilation of spiritual biographies adorned my desk.

The very next morning I began my now longtime practice of reading Butler's entries for the saints whose feasts fell on that day, seeking advice, encouragement, and some reason to keep putting one foot in front of the other. What I found was all that, and more. Soon I was buying additional books by or about holy men and women whose lives especially interested me. Widowed saints in particular proved a revelation. There were so many of them, and when their husbands died, they'd been outsiders in their times and places far beyond what I could imagine. Nevertheless, they'd dusted themselves off, relied on God, and discovered new (often incredibly inventive and impressive) ways of serving. The holy widow was not a rare phenomenon but a giant sisterhood, I discovered, a sisterhood to which any widow might aspire if she relied on God for help.[11]

This new morning routine brought God more explicitly into the familiar teaching sphere, too. Events and conversations at work echoed saints' stories I'd read, encouraging reflection on the commonalities of human experience and softening judgment on my part. Encountering people in need, I found myself thinking of saints I'd met whose lives had offered similar hurdles and praying for their intercession . . . and thus building a habit of praying throughout the day. The saints provided practical examples, modeling in parallel contexts how a person of good will might deal more thoughtfully and faith-fully with anxious students, difficult colleagues, and intervals of flagging energy.

Nine months into this fruitful practice, I woke in the night in the grip of what felt like a bizarre imperative: my next book would be a collection of reflections for teachers based on the lives of the saints.

I stared at the ceiling, incredulous. I'd never written anything like that. And who was I to undertake such a project given my imperfect understanding of Christianity, my wavering faith . . . not to say that it was *very* early days in my relationship with the saints? Seriously: *Get thee behind me, ego . . . or devil . . . or temporary wild impulse.*

But a first essay would not stop yelling at me in the dark, whole phrases and structure bursting into sudden life. With sleep impossible, I turned on the light and jotted notes on a bedside notepad. What I saw in the morning moved me to transcribe those scribbles onto the computer, and over the next few days that initial chapter seemed to write itself. Another followed, then a book proposal, which was accepted. Within two years I was receiving royalty checks, hearing from readers, invited to speak on the radio and at teachers' conferences.

Nobody was more surprised than me when I became a "Catholic writer." Yet *My Best Teachers Were Saints* pointed me in a direction that still feels like exactly where I'm supposed to be going.

But that grace-filled direction, it appears in retrospect, was just the warm-up, the "starter annunciation" for the paradigm-busting call that turned my primary employment from headwork to literal handwork, and me from someone phobic about illness and death, who didn't like being touched by anyone except her nearest and dearest, into a woman who is comfortable with laying healing hands on total strangers.

So how did God engineer *that?* Once again, gradually and tactfully, by placing hard to miss signs in the path, by making sure that path was smooth enough that I dared to try treading it.

In this case the initial nudge came *way* in advance of more overt prompting, and thus simmered in my heart for a good long while. It happened even earlier than the hint about the saints, predating Ford's death by six months, when a nurse-neighbor came on her own accord to our house to offer my husband palliative massage ("healing touch," she called it, though it was intended to ease pain and to comfort rather than to cure that terminal disease). Ford and I had been skeptical, but he shrugged and said, "What can it hurt?" And she *was* our respected colleague and trusted friend, so we'd agreed. To our surprise the touch of her healing hands did provide significant relief for my husband. And to my even greater surprise, when she insisted that I take a turn, I discovered that I too could feel the dark energy of Ford's pain ease as I followed her instructions.

Paralyzed by hopelessness in the months that followed, I did not repeat the experiment. Yet so odd was that experience of delivering relief through my hands, and so counter to the way I had always thought of myself, that it never completely faded from my mind. In fact, as retirement from my teaching career neared, the idea of healing touch kept thrusting itself forward as a possible answer to that "writing all day alone in your house" problem. It seemed I might have a gift for this type of healing massage, I told myself, and such things ought to be explored. By then the "making something good out of tragedy" idea had become a mental commitment, and the more I thought about it, the more laying compassionate hands on the dying, their caregivers, and the bereaved seemed a particularly appropriate possibility for honoring my husband's memory. Perhaps

I might offer to do such a thing a few times a month, I imagined, through church or other connections.

So, just for the heck of it, I checked out the practicalities of offering therapeutic touch to strangers, learned I'd need a state massage license, and discovered that *it just so happened* that my university's vocational/technical branch offered the necessary training. I took a career exploration class, then committed to one preliminary course each semester around the edges of my teaching, feeling my enthusiasm and commitment getting stronger all the time. Things flowed as if they were meant to be . . . and immediately after I retired, I enrolled in the massage therapy program's yearlong clinical component.

That year as a vocational technical student in the massage therapy certificate program proved so challenging—and so good for me, reinforcing what the past decade had taught about persisting and learning through difficulties, adjusting, keeping the faith, taking one's time, and listening. At first I struggled with rote memorization; I asked *way* too many questions for the teachers' taste. I was awkward in my touch, employing too much or too little pressure, working in the wrong spots, using the wrong techniques. I felt socially awkward, too, among my fresh-out-of-high-school classmates, who initially kept their distance from the 63-year-old "professor," giggling in groups while I sat alone, choosing me last for partner. But the sense of calling sustained me. If I could live through early widowhood, I assured myself, I could learn this craft and cultivate these kiddos' friendship. So I did what I'd learned to do by then—observe, reflect, study, empathetically read my classmates, and pray about all of the above, shrugging off disappointments and trying again, trusting that if I was supposed to be doing this, a way would open. And it did.

Besides providing knowledge and affirming my social skills, that year also reinforced my growing sense that intuition, inflected by faith, was a seriously important way of knowing. As I relaxed and got out of my own way, I began to feel my hands move in ways I hadn't planned, guided by what felt like an inspired, wordless energy that was both me and not-me . . . an energy that was always right, and invariably helpful. Gone was the academic me who had inevitably privileged her logical, analytical powers above any other tool. In massage school the instructors spoke of "positive energy" and "Reiki spirit guides"; from my Christian perspective, I've come to understand this force as an emanation of the Holy Spirit using me in its service, a wise force that willingly partners with me, so long as I stay open to accepting its presence.

I emerged from massage school a different person than the Susan who went in, full of new knowledge and technique, less wedded to a strictly rational mindset, more empathetic with people not like me, fully reconciled to the fact that learning would necessarily keep evolving and surprises would inevitably keep happening.

Right after graduation—having long made up my mind that I wanted to do more than a few random massages a month—I established Balsamroot Massage in a spare room in an old house where an acquaintance had an interior design business. Clients started coming; it was an exciting time. Not long after, *the* giant glorious surprise arrived, as a geriatrician I knew from church (the above-mentioned Dr. Morris) got wind of the kind of work I was doing and invited me to work with her hospice group as an independent contractor. For over a decade now, I've treated a dozen clients per week in my studio and two dozen hospice patients and caregivers every month in homes and facilities across eastern Idaho, feeling my hands ease shoulders cramped from weeks in bed, reduce painful edema in swollen legs, draw smiles and coherent words from people with dementia, and comfort widows and widowers as devastated as I once was.

All shall be well, these hands proclaim as I do that work—and proclaim it with utmost confidence, I might add. For after the history of calling I've just recited, it seems to me impossible to imagine that this world of ours works in any other way.

+ + +

Just the other Saturday I hiked in the national forest near my home with a friend who's in the midst of accepting and mapping her own radical redirection. Now in her mid-thirties, Bridget has lived an adventuresome life as a world traveler, professional musician, freelance editor/writer, museum docent, perennial student, then settled five years ago into a career as a university music professor alongside her new husband, while deftly handling raising a toddler daughter and the care and maintenance of several student woodwind ensembles.

Then the couple's second child, a little boy, was born prematurely at 23 weeks. Needless to say, many of Billy's little systems weren't fully developed, his lungs and digestive system being particularly worrisome. Billy spent the first year of his life in the NICU of a children's hospital experiencing crisis after crisis, his anguished parents taking turns at his side.

But that little guy has been blessed with an undauntable spirit and great zest for life, and two years ago he came home to stay. Now he's walking, talking, laughing, charming, and romping (his musical destiny appears to be the drums). But he's still on supplemental oxygen, is dangerously susceptible to infections, and needs regular check-ins with his doctors, so Bridget has taken an extended leave of absence from the university. This once actively curious wanderer's time is now spent almost entirely within her home's confines, her attention focused on her son.

As we ease into each other's company on the hike's steep uphill half, we remark mostly on the scenery—aspens greening up with spring, cranes offering their energetic gargling calls from nests hidden down along the creek, clouds soaring on gusty winds above the mountaintop. But once the comparative ease of descent lightens our breathing and opens our lips, the talk gets more serious. Bridget asks me about the past month's massage sessions and my writing projects, then laughingly describes her little ones' fussy eating, restless sleeping, and tendency to scatter toys everywhere. She also confesses the soul-deep satisfaction this new closeness to her children offers, admitting that she might not want to go back to teaching after all, once Billy's health stabilizes.

Then she shares news I've not heard before, announcing that she's approached the children's hospital that treated Billy about organizing a peer counseling service for parents of critically ill infants. "We needed so much help," she says. "The kind of help you wouldn't know you need unless you've been through it—logistical, informational, emotional."

She was a little nervous about contacting the administrators, Bridget admits, but everybody thought the idea wonderful, and they agreed that when Billy's condition allows, she should lead the planning sessions and chair the eventual oversight board. "'Just tell us what you need," they promised. Bridget is already brainstorming, ordering books, considering participants. "But that's in the future," she says. "Right now, I'm so boring!" I shake my head no, laughing.

Bridget and I are not people who would have ever anticipated—or remotely imagined—that we'd be doing what we're doing at this point in life, and no doubt the scars that propelled us in these new directions still show. Nevertheless, we're both standing straight as we pause on that mountain trail, smiling at each other, knowing that the other is in her own way very happy with that present moment—one that's been imposed on her, yes, but one in whose unfolding creation she's willingly participating.

Angels are not regarding us with wonder as we walk together, insofar as we can see.

But the God of love and annunciation walks with us.

Alessandro Allori, *The Annunciation*, 1603.

Chapter Four

The Annunciations of Later Years

Aging with Creative Equanimity

As in so many Renaissance paintings of the annunciation, Alessandro Allori's 1603 Mary has turned away from Gabriel upon hearing his proclamation, amazed and seeking space to take it in. Her hands are raised palms-out in the conventional gesture of surprise; her eyes are downcast. Gabriel regards her response intently, as he does in numerous other paintings, hovering at stage left with his right hand raised commandingly.

If you look closer at the details, though, you'll notice subtle differences from the usual conventions of *conturbatio* renderings. Allori's Mary is neither stunned in her countenance like Fra Angelico's, nor panicking and rebellious in kinetic movement like Lotto's, but much more composed in her body language. This is a woman with some gravitas—as indicated by the luxurious material of her dress, the elaborate pillow, and the golden threads on her bobbin-lace loom—a woman who might even be smiling the barest hint of a perturbed, self-aware smile. She stands calmly with stable balance, grounded on her own two firmly planted, rather substantial feet, at rest rather than trying to get away. Her raised hands are not pointing toward the angel, attempting to fend him off, but out at the viewer, seeming to invite commiseration. Those hands register surprise, certainly, but the fingertips are tilted outward at the top, forming a kind of flared open-bowl shape that makes a space for the light behind her to come down, accepting her role as Jesus' mother even as she attempts to wrap her mind around what's going on.

I'll admit that I smiled the first time I encountered Alessandro Allori's Mary in the Accademia Museum, having returned to Florence a decade after that sad solo pilgrimage of 2004. Actually, I chuckled out loud. A man glanced nervously at me; a couple turned and moved to the next painting . . . *crazy woman.* And that was a reasonable response—for who in her right mind would laugh at an image of the Virgin Mary caught in a grave moment of disquiet, a woman perturbed and asking, "How can this be?"

What had inspired such behavior that day in fact was good old identification, though not the kind of weighty projection this book has discussed in earlier chapters. The connection that made me laugh that day was avocation-inspired; rather than flowing from all those big questions about obedience and agency, it was sparked by a small scene-setting detail: the bobbin-lace loom in the picture's lower left corner.

In and of itself that loom is worthy of attention on multiple levels, as such details often are in great art. The object is a delightfully detailed touch, its careful rendering reflecting Allori's interest in fiber arts.[1] It also carries symbolic weight, reminding us that Mary is a "maker" in multiple senses. The lace fabric's intricate structure evinces her considerable skill, patience, and ability to follow a pattern, and the expensive golden thread implies that this is not a woman working for a modest living but someone who's drawn to creative work for the pure joy of creating.

It was none of those reflection-worthy insights, though, that made me laugh that day, but a blast of amused, particular insight as a fellow fiber arts enthusiast. If you too are among our tribe, you'll surely relate to what's implied by the loom's position right next to Mary's chair, and by its dangling bobbins: this cosmos-changing moment has arrived, inconveniently, just when its star player is absorbed in the complex craft of lacemaking. Every serious crafter, I trust, will identify with that situation as I did, for it seems that there's never enough time to pursue one's art. Even when you think you've managed to steal a blissful hour, some interloper or phone call, some pet making a mess, some household emergency, some domestic obligation suddenly remembered, trespasses on the precious time. Given such context, Mary's raised hands might be read as a gesture of frustration!

Oh, girlfriend, I get what you're feeling, I'd thought a millisecond before that laugh. *Just when the flow is happening, just as you've recovered your place in the pattern or realized exactly what you want to do with the design, some darned angel inevitably comes along and butts in with something that has to be done* now. *It never ends, does it?*

Allori himself would have been abundantly familiar with such interruptions to the creative process. As the longtime master of a large workshop, he surely would have weathered untimely demands for his attention over the years while he himself tried to paint ("Sorry to bother you, Sir, but the apprentice Giovanni has just fallen off the scaffold!" or "I thought we had more lapis lazuli before they started work on the fresco today, Master, but we're out, and he's right in the middle of Mary's gown!"). Obviously, since he'd long been a major artist and director of an extensive and very successful business, Allori had learned to accept and cope with such interruptions . . . but "coping" and getting to the point where they no longer annoyed him are very different things.

At the time Allori created this evocative Annunciation, moreover, an infinitely more serious, non-negotiable "interruption" in his career—his own mortality—would have been much on his mind. An aged man in 1603, Allori must have been aware of his rapidly declining health; just a few years later he would die. Once among Florence's most prolific and respected painters, Allori was by then delegating to his son an increasingly greater share of the work of managing the studio, and of executing its most important paintings.

Nevertheless, the elder Allori hadn't given up on his own talent or creative energy but kept on painting, producing in his old age works of stunning technique and complex nuance, including this one. "All you can do is roll with it," he might have said if he'd been a painter of the Beat poets' Zen-inflected era, perhaps with a hint of a resigned smile.

One Italian art critic has speculated that Allori might not have been the only person in this painting's story who was thinking about interruptions in a life path, specifically the disruptions that aging brings. While we don't know who commissioned this 1603 Annunciation or for whom, the fact that this painting was later acquired by a museum from a private suite in a Medici palace hints that it might have been created with an aging Medici matriarch in mind. Perhaps the prominence of that bobbin-lace loom indicates that she was a passionate practitioner of that craft herself. Perhaps, as Allori created this image as a focus for private prayer in the rooms to which that woman was increasingly confined, he was inviting her to claim kinship with this particular image of the Mother of God.[2]

Admittedly, we'll never know if such a woman, "elderly" by the world's standards, once drew on Allori's Mary to cultivate her peace with the changes God was working in her life, even to remind herself that amused resignation was the only really healthy way to weather the accumulating "annunciations" of old age. But I can tell you one thing with absolute assurance: thanks to the contemporary availability of high-quality framed art prints, such a woman *does* exist today.

It's me.

The Unavoidable Changes of Aging

"Every other week it's something," my massage patient complains, throwing her hands in the air in a gesture eerily reminiscent of the one in the image I contemplated just two hours before. "This past summer it was that osteoporosis diagnosis, then losing our senior dog, and our old furnace giving out, and then, just as I'm getting used to cutting back on salt, they tell me I'm not supposed to drive at night anymore. This getting old just isn't fair."

I don't even try to console her but simply nod, for I too have been lately lamenting signs pointing to a personal change of season. In my case things aren't quite that dire, for I'm still able to walk four or five miles in the national forest almost every day, work in a job that requires physical stamina, and look forward to the next writing project. But younger companions like Bridget now frequently have to wait for me when trails turn uphill, I need more sleep to function, and on occasion I forget why I've gone into a room. I've also been shocked to find myself patronized by people who don't know me, most recently called "dear" by a new doctor who patted me and asked how many times a week I fall (once in the past year, thank you very much, when I hit an icy patch on a cross-country ski run appropriately named "Screamer"). Much worse, some old friendships are flagging as former companions and I find ourselves without the conversation-starters our shared work once provided, as people move away to be near grandchildren, as our collective energy for socializing wanes.

Such concerns, however, seem minor compared to what my patient now confesses. "But the worst thing," she admits, "landed last week. Tests showed the arthritis that crippled my mother is getting worse in me, fast. They can try to address it, but it seems pretty certain that my hands, my knees, my neck, and my shoulders are going to get all crippled up, and I won't be able to work in the garden anymore." I wince, thinking of her beautiful yard, the demonstration classes she offers at the local greenhouse and at high schools, the glorious bouquets of dahlias, roses, and gladiolas that she donates to weddings, funerals, hospitals, and nursing homes.

She regards me with a gaze at once plaintive and terrified. "And what am I going to do if I can't work in the garden?"

A good question indeed, one that in some form or other so many of us will find ourselves asking . . . a genre not unfamiliar to me. *What am I going to do if something happens to my legs and balance, and I can't walk in the mountains? How will I function if I lose my hearing and can't calm and inspire myself with music?* And most frightening of all: *How will I go on living if I lose my sight and can't write or knit or live independently?*

When such useless panic swells and I'm at home, I go out in the hall and contemplate my soul-sister Mary, as imagined in Allori's painting. She reminds me that, while it's natural to have these little moments of anticipatory alarm, I need to regain some perspective, fast. What remotely constructive choice do we have, after all, but to trust that some now-mysterious good will be made bright at last from the past's wreckage (or from the utter confusion of the pattern we thought was progressing so well)? *You don't necessarily have to like it,* I've imagined her comforting me, *you just have to make peace with it. And sometimes, all you can do is laugh.*

Aging as "A New Stage of Life"

My imagined Mary is far from the only one, you'll be aware, who has used humor to defuse the slings and arrows of aging. Jokes abound that laugh not at the old themselves but communally at the tribulations of aging ("How is the moon like dentures? Both come out at night!" or "One benefit of old age is that your secrets are always safe with your friends . . . because they can't remember them!"). Humor theorists have explained that when such a joke undercuts an assumed script (or schema), it humbles us as we smile at our own mistaken assumptions.[3] "Humor brings us back down to earth and reminds us of our place in God's universe," James Martin writes.[4]

Sad to say, however, it's despair, not healthy laughter, that seems so often the norm for senior citizens. So many I serve during my massage rounds appear to have given up on themselves, surrendering their interest in doing much of anything beyond enduring and lamenting. Even when opportunities for stimulation and fellowship do exist, a surprising number decline, as is the case in the large and enlightened nursing home where my mother lives in Pennsylvania. So many activities are offered there, including talks, concerts, church services, a bridge club, puzzles, a library, exercise and art classes. Yet the events are more often than not sparsely attended; the same few people repeatedly patronize the library and classes. Administrators at a large assisted-living home where I provide hospice massages have an even sadder story to tell. When they collaborated with a charter school to arrange weekly sessions for second graders to practice their reading with residents, interest was so scant that the project soon proved unviable.

Instead, so many seasoned adults with potentially so much love, advice, prayer, and friendship to offer spend their days alone, disengaged from the world. The Christian perspective on old age imagines such a different scenario—a life-giving scenario of which so many seem tragically unaware. Benedictine Sister Joan Chittister's book, *The Gift of Years: Growing Older Gracefully,* sums it up thus: "The last phase of life is not non-life [but] a *new* stage of life. . . . Old age enlightens—not simply ourselves, as important as that may be, but those around us as well."[5] While not denying age's challenges and sorrows, Chittister explains that old age offers its own *unique* possibilities for contributing to the world's peace, and for spiritual, emotional, and intellectual personal growth. No longer tied to the regimentation of a regular job, nor feeling pressure to build a career and find worldly success, older people are free to ask new questions, experiment, slow down, pray, and celebrate God's creation. And aging's very limitations, distressing though they might be, introduce opportunities for faithful ones to open their eyes to the world's needs and their own potential. Physical restrictions beckon the aging to explore new and long-neglected interests that don't involve so much physical effort. Solitude and open-ended days invite the lonely to seek new community by reaching out to others. As Chittister writes, "A burden of these years is the temptation to cling to the times and things behind us rather than move to the liberating moments ahead. A blessing of these years is the invitation to go light-footed into the here and now—because we spend far too much of life preparing for the future rather than enjoying the present."

One avenue of invitation Chittister particularly emphasizes is the opportunity to grow closer to God. In chapters titled "Transformation," "Mystery," "Religion," "Spirituality," and "Faith," she explains that the simple fact of being forced to confront weakness, lack of control, and mortality encourages a person to draw nearer to God. Invited by slower days to spend more time appreciating the beauty in ordinary days and objects, in human friendship, in prayers, written words, and liturgies of faith, we can foster within us the practice of gratitude. Moved by the passing years to review the trajectories of our lives, we can appreciate how the Mystery has been shaping, encouraging, and coaching us all along.

What a gift this perspective offers in a secular culture whose stereotypes of aging are inevitably depressing . . . what a breath of fresh air and an inspiration for all who long for lives that are meaningful throughout their span.

Stages of Aging: Green Old Age

"Old age," of course, is not a monolith but a succession of mini-seasons, each with its own gifts and limitations. In the three-part division most common in the literature of geriatric science, the earliest of those stages begins after retirement in people's mid-sixties and lasts into their seventies. "Young old age," it's often termed, but I prefer the more poetic term "green old age" (as this stage of life was called in England and America from 1500–1700) with its metaphor of fresh growth. Green old age denotes people who are slowing down with fewer responsibilities, but who are still mentally and physically active and able to live independently. Marked by new freedom, it invites those who traverse it to tap into talents previously put on hold, discover new or unimagined capabilities, take healthy and heady leaps into interesting and attractive unknowns.

Green old age can be a very happy time of life; indeed, research suggests that many people consider the years immediately post-retirement as among their best. One Duke University/National Institutes on Aging study documented that happiness levels generally rise during ages 64–74 from what they were between ages 60–64, and even from the early middle-aged "prime of life." Explanations for this phenomenon come easily to mind, for green old age offers discretion to schedule congenial avocations and leisure, comparative lack of workplace pressure and stress, and reduced childrearing responsibilities. With greater awareness of time's passing, people in this age group report that they also feel freer to divest themselves of things that don't satisfy and substitute activities and people that do.[6]

This is not to say, of course, that everybody necessarily finds green old age a period of fulfillment. Those who face health challenges and those strapped for financial resources, in particular, are less likely to experience a rise in "happiness levels" during this time (a subject whose implications for faith is complex enough for another book).

Even those who seem to have everything a retired person could want might find themselves adrift for at least a time. While initially the newly liberated might boast of sleeping in and the joy of totally unstructured time or daily golf, after a while boredom can become a problem. "Sometimes I feel invisible," a woman who once couldn't wait for retirement confessed to me after two glasses of wine. "This is fun, but it's not really a life." *Aha!* Henri Nouwen might say. *That's a sign! It's time to start listening for God's direction!*

It is possible, of course, to avoid (or delay, at least) such questions of meaning by launching oneself immediately into a "second-act career," as many people do these days. Some newly retired folks undertake alternate professions, as I have; others repurpose extant skills in new contexts as volunteers. Examples of the latter abound in my cohort, which includes two retired dentists who travel as volunteers to Central and South America to minister to children; a former prosecuting attorney who works as a court-appointed official advocate for children-at-risk; and the former director of our county's public social service agency who in retirement employs her organizational skills, gentle but firm leadership style, knowledge of community needs and resources, and well-honed talent for hearing others out as she chairs our parish council.

Then there's Margot, whom God "surprised" into extending her career skills just when she assumed she might let them get a little dusty. An exemplary teacher of severely disabled preschool children, Margot was understandably looking forward to "vegging out, traveling, and relaxing" in retirement. Soon after she retired, however, financial circumstances forced her daughter to join the ranks of the employed. Being a responsible woman devoted to her family, Margot accepted that she was being called to step in to care for her two toddler grandchildren, a double handful of exuberant energy that would have been daunting to any woman of her age. For several years Margot has spent every weekday with those little ones, and what a gift she's been to them, and they to her. Drawing on her vast repertoire of enriching and fun activities, and on her well-honed understanding of the stages of child development and quirks of toddler behavior, Margot's grandchildren are so ahead of the curve, so secure, so happy that one can only grin to see them. Margot's social media posts of their daily activities glow with joy; her connection with her daughter has deepened. What some might consider a burden has become a blessing.

But you don't have to "work" to find meaning in green old age, of course, for leisure, prayerfully practiced, can also become a gift to the world. My friend Anne, who labored for many years in the accounting office of a large federal agency, presents a sterling example of such truly "green" old age. After she and her husband retired, the broadly curious Anne joined an adult continuing education group, determined to explore hobbies and interests her work schedule had previously prevented her from enjoying. For the past few years she's been working enthusiastically through the organization's extensive catalog of classes—stained glass, woodworking, knitting, pottery, cooking, lectures on history, health, the arts, geology, and wildflowers. She's also joined the local Project Linus group, a sewing circle that makes quilts for hospitalized children and the homeless.

Always a charitable person, Anne is finding particular satisfaction in this latter activity. Yet even in her purely recreational activities, sharing her cheerful, friendly nature has turned retirement into a season of generous giving. While Anne's kindness has always been clear to her friends, now a much wider audience reaps its benefits. She invites people to talk about themselves, extends a hand of friendship to those who are lonely, encourages those who doubt their ability to perform or understand a course's content, and enthusiastically admires what others make or say. "This was always a nice group," I heard someone say recently about the Project Linus meetings, "but it's welcoming on a whole new level since Anne's joined us."

Green old age can also unfold happily and productively in more private spheres. That's taking place for Julie, a former student of mine who's welcomed her aging parents into her rambling old house in a country town, which I visit every few weeks to offer hospice massages to the older couple. Both are declining; Julie's mother's dementia is increasing, and her father is growing extremely frail physically, his death clearly approaching. But I've never walked into a happier, more loving home—a kind of paradise of what a family ought to be, one that also includes Julie's grown daughter and her toddler son, and two affectionate, large rescue dogs. Julie has worked as a professional in several fields, lived in big, hip cities, traveled abroad. Yet there's no hint of boredom or impatience in that house, where multiple generations are happily absorbed in the daily business of nurturing one another. Julie seems infused with a radiant sense of purpose I don't remember ever sensing in her as a college student.

Fulfilling though such green old age callings can be, it's crucial to remember that they're no more likely to be permanent safe harbors for meaning than a person's previous occupation. Before long Julie's parents will go to God, and she'll need to find other activities or service to absorb the time and energy she's now devoting to them. In the coming years, Margot's grandchildren will start school. Anne and her husband both have health conditions that, while now well-controlled, might make it difficult to keep up that happy round of continuing education in the future.

As I write this, I'm also thinking about a major source of my own sense of meaning in green old age—the studio massage component of the work I do several days a week. This "regular" (aka non-hospice) massage is very satisfying, and I've made many friends, but for about a year I've caught myself feeling like it's trespassing on my writing time. Creative leisure is calling, too. I drive to work while longing to stop along the way and offer a "sacrifice of praise" through reverent noticing, like going down to the river to watch the flotillas of fluffy baby geese with their protective parents, or hiking up the hillside to sit in the first golden aspen grove of fall. I've been wishing for more time with my dear friends Anne and Bridget, and with the former graduate student who has become in every way that matters my "daughter," Shelley. I daydream about more time to read and study, to knit, to take those voice lessons that would make me more of an asset to Sunday's music ministry, to hear myself think and talk to God.

If not now, when? What would it be like to close the studio and just continue hospice work? Am I finally ready, psychologically and spiritually, to accept that I'm a worthy child of God in the absence of explicit, daily, reinforcing feedback that says, *You're appreciated* or *You're valuable?*

The answer, my discernment suggests, is a strong "maybe." On the social side, I have good friends always glad to do something together, so I'm hardly doomed to be a hermit. Yet I'll admit that what I crave most these days is reflective solitude. As my writing has become more niched, others are arguably "with" me on those days anyway, for I consult imagined readers while picking up and turning over ideas, trying to imagine what concepts will be most useful to them, what writing strategies might encourage reflection. Far from a "lonely widow sitting in her house all day," I've learned to be happy in my own company—indeed, to long for it on the occasions when in-person interaction becomes noisy and protracted. "Almost monastic," a friend lately termed the way I live in the stretches when I'm home alone. Since she's a highly sociable person, I'm not sure she meant it as a good thing, but I heard my internal voice enthusiastically say, *Exactly!*

Still, I want to get this decision—which still feels quite daring, like a final, decisive cutting of the cord of "householder-dom"—

right, so I'm taking my time, listening and praying and taking my emotional temperature when I'm on my own for an extended period, coming up with strategies for how I might ensure regular, in-person fellowship with friends.

But you know what? That once essential everyday reinforcement that I am "somebody" now feels much less essential, and the possibility of unearthing more free time feels more exhilarating, and more right, every day.

Stages of Aging: Old-Old Age

When the second stage of old age arrives—old-old age, where physical/mental complaints arise or multiply or worsen, and living independently becomes more difficult or impossible—that "if not now, when" question obviously takes on greater weight. By their mid-eighties, many if not most people rely at least in part on paid caregivers or loving, hardworking family members for help with the basic activities of daily life. Health concerns and medical treatments change daily routines. Separation from a familiar home may become necessary; the fact of mortality becomes harder to ignore. Yet this stage, too, offers its own proper work—work that involves proportionately less "doing" and more "being."

For, as Chittister explains, the season of accruing years and increasing limitations is an ideal time to explore and share inner gifts, including compassion and curiosity about others. Pope Francis—an aged man himself and one committed to fostering respect for the elderly—has repeatedly suggested that such sharing might especially take place as the elderly connect with and nurture the young. The experience of so many elderly people I know, including Margot, confirms the wisdom of that recommendation, as they speak with joy of time spent with children, grandchildren, other people's children, young friends who come to visit them for talks and advice, homework help, cooking lessons, memory-sharing, or mutual craft sessions (as in the case of an elderly woman I know who hosts a well-attended drop-in "learn to crochet" party at her home for her grandchildren and their friends, her young neighbors, etc., every other Sunday afternoon).

Even when an elderly person is disabled or unable to communicate well verbally, the possibility for such connection with younger people is inherent in the caregiving situation itself, Francis has explained. When the elderly allow others to care for them, caregivers receive an opportunity to discover wells of empathy within themselves, to practice love incarnate. And when the person being cared for is able to offer any expression of thanks at all—even a smile or a hand squeeze—it reinforces the holy sense that it is good, indeed, to be here on this earth together.[7]

Social interaction that reminds the elderly that they are still important and cherished can also be a component of another recommendation Francis has made for the elderly: that they spend time actively seeking God. I know several elderly people who now attend their longtime Bible study groups via Zoom; one hosts the in-person version of that meeting every six months in an activity room in her nursing home. Most parishes have ministries to the homebound and elderly, and such visitors seem most often to be people in the green old age season, so these ministries do double duty service to the aging. I've also seen faith-sharing flourish on a more private level through the "religious book club" one of my hospice patients in her early nineties and her three daughters maintain. The four of them sit down with someone's laptop, browse a Catholic publisher's website, and choose a book they want to read together, then enjoy sharing reactions, faith . . . and, of course, cake.

My friend Pat, for whom I offered weekly hospice massages for several years, provided one of the best demonstrations imaginable of how an old-old person might follow Francis's advice to transform what could have been a lonely, bitter time into a period of unique late-in-life flourishing. A lively, broadly curious mother of two who'd put herself through college after an early divorce and owned a successful needlework shop, Pat was crushed to find that worsening heart and lung problems mandated a move into assisted-living care at age 83. But the blessings of a devoted daughter who lived nearby, an excellent nursing home, continued mental acuity, and deep trust that God still had use for her allowed Pat to do just as she'd always wished: "to live right up until I die." Her active faith was supported by visits from priests and eldercare ministers. She streamed Mass daily on her iPad. She continued learning, too, employing that device to read the books she'd always meant to read and to "visit" museums and "attend" symphony concerts. She cultivated a little indoor garden of the exotic succulents she'd always admired.

This was not merely a period of self-cultivation, though. Pat possessed a robust gift for fellowship, and dedicated herself to building close personal friendships with her caregivers, many of whom were college students majoring in health professions. When the facility's employees came into her room, she'd ask about them instead of lamenting her own circumstances, and in her friendly, sympathetic presence these young women gradually opened up, confessing struggles, hopes, fears, dreams, sorrows. Pat listened, commiserated, observed, offered advice when it was requested, spoke candidly of herself when asked. Before long the young people were spending their breaks with her. She remembered birthdays and graduations; she shared books and proofread college papers; she taught one of her caregivers to become a master gardener of indoor plants, another the basics of embroidery (as she had so many others in her needlework shop).

When Pat died many eyes were red from the loss of a true friend; but at the same time many lives had been set on surer paths, including mine. And in the end, she left not only a personal legacy, but one with long-term implications, for Pat's example had taught her young caregivers that an elderly person could be as distinctive, as varied and quirky, as full of surprising talents and interests as anybody else—and as precious a friend. She'd made the elderly "real people" for those aspiring nurses, teaching them what questions to ask, priming them to look for commonalities and insight instead of just making assumptions—a perspective surely destined to enrich the lives of all the future patients those young women will tend.

Stages of Aging: The Approach of Death as a Time for Reconciliation

The final period of old age, as death draws near, offers its own unique challenges . . . and its own unique opportunities. It's the premier occasion in human life when denial will get us nowhere—though some do attempt to deny right up until the end, as did one of my patients who elected to endure two separate courses of chemotherapy after her 94th birthday. But attempting to say "no" at the eleventh hour is ultimately a fool's game, an empty gambit which robs the dying of their last chance to make peace with the greatest, most important disruption of them all.

As I discuss such matters, I want to be clear that my own "hope is built on nothing less" (as a classic hymn about grace says[8]) than the proposition that a loving God will indeed bear us creatures up as we pass into whatever comes next . . . that ultimately we have nothing to fear, as hard as that might be to imagine when we, or those we love best, are dying. Lately, indeed, I've been hearing the phrase "all who have died in your mercy" in the eucharistic prayer at Mass, with an emphasis on that "all," and thinking of it as very broadly inclusive indeed. Our faith insists, after all, that our God is a God of mercy, a God who never stops hoping—and intending—for all of us to enjoy salvation in our creator's presence. "The Lord is waiting to be gracious to you, truly, he shall rise to show you mercy," Isaiah says (30:18).

I've also been spending time with the writing of the theologian Origen (who lived from about 185–253), a man who professes that given God's fundamental grace, everyone can have hope of coming home to God. It's true that Origen was judged a heretic two centuries after his death—but he's been widely defended by mainstream theologians since, including Pope Benedict XVI. Those who do so emphasize that such a position is not incompatible with punishment for sins, and that Origen himself wrote that although salvation might be inevitable in the fullness of time, it will not take place for anyone until his purification is complete.[9] What's ultimately mandatory in Origen's equation is that we each submit of our own free will, acknowledging that God ultimately and properly holds sovereignty, not we ourselves.

Salvation, in other words, depends on a person learning to say "yes" with all her mind, all her heart, all her soul.

Deathbeds are, of course, a classic venue for the acceptance of such salvific grace (indeed, the whole "inevitable" situation appears to encourage surrender of will). You'll have heard, read, or seen on film plenty of stories describing deathbed conversions, often marked by weeping and shouting, perhaps featuring dying souls who testify to hearing angel choirs or seeing the hand of God reaching toward them.

Far be it from me to discount such episodes. But there are other ways that such bending toward God can take place, ways that occur more gradually as the dying heed Hosea's advice to "plow up the hard ground of your hearts, for now is the time to seek the LORD, that he may come and shower righteousness upon you" (10:12, NLT). Though less dramatic than last-minute conversions, such inner turnings toward God are more common and, I'd argue, equally worth celebrating. For no less than glad shouts or effusive tears, a subtle increase in kindness, a new willingness to forgive, a heart more open to divine whisperings, constitute signs that defenses are breaking down and holy love has been invited into these souls—that on some level that essential "yes" is being said, if not aloud.

As this book ends, I want to sketch the embodiment of that process that lies closest to my heart, the sequence of events that occurred as my own husband unclenched his hands from long-term resistance and turned receptively toward Mystery in a process that infused his last weeks on earth with light . . . a process that has made it possible for me to imagine my life's own conclusion with less fear.

It wasn't that Ford was a crusading atheist or that he knew nothing about religion—far from it. He was instead one of those innately spiritual and ethical (even reverent) people who, for a long time, simply couldn't make his peace with the injustices and brutality so prevalent in the history of organized religion, or with what he judged to be the intolerant self-righteousness and hypocrisy of some contemporary churches. Raised Episcopalian, as an adolescent Ford had abandoned altar-serving for Sundays in the Virginia woods that lifted his soul; as a college student he'd acquired a freethinker's disdain for those who did what their ecclesiastical leaders told them to do even when it seemed to contradict the faith. He professed no explicit creed but kindness and a sense of ethics, tolerance, reverence for the created world, and what the poet John Keats termed "negative capability," the capacity to rest in agnostic uncertainty about what religions taught.

Despite such professed skepticism, Ford had always seemed drawn to faith. He didn't object to my Catholicism—indeed, he applauded my conversion a few years after we married. He knew a great deal about Christian theology, and about Judaism, and Buddhism, and Hinduism, and Confucianism, and so on. He loved the music of faith (from Bach's cantatas to The Stanley Brothers' bluegrass gospel) and was drawn to literature that concerned itself with questions of meaning, immanent presence, good and evil (John Milton, William Wordsworth, T. S. Eliot, Gary Snyder). Such themes were prevalent in his own poems, too—to the extent that several were solicited for a volume titled *Pacific Northwest Spiritual Poetry* (their publication made him smile). I'd learned early, though, that a direct approach to turning his heart would be counterproductive, as evinced by his flaring anger one Christmas Eve when I'd pressured him into going to Mass with our friends after a festive dinner.

Thus it surprised me when, shortly after the cancer diagnosis, he was the one who cracked open the door of faith by suggesting that we travel to "our beach" on the Washington State coast for a roll-your-own spiritual retreat. For the span of a long weekend, we spent afternoons sitting in the dunes above a remote stretch of surf, trying to convey what we each believed. I was still nervous about pushing too hard then, and I've often wished since that I'd been clearer in my own mind and more articulate that weekend. Nevertheless, my husband's willingness to consider my beliefs was clear.

A few months later I returned from teaching a night class to find Ford propped up in bed, absorbed in his grandfather's Book of Common Prayer. No comment (though a little embarrassment was evident that first time, as if he'd been caught). Soon, though, that volume found a place in plain view on the bedside table.

During Ford's final year of life, it seemed that his faith was growing stronger as mine ebbed. He became adamant about my going to Mass, though public worship at that time felt like a trial, with everyone hovering and the words striking me as empty cant. Some Sundays I just pretended to attend but instead whiled away an hour in a coffee shop—though I always made sure to review the readings beforehand, for my husband had taken to scanning my lectionary and was apt to inquire about the homily. The poems Ford was writing for what would be his last, prize-winning book themselves testify to dawning belief, expressing as they do a yearning to believe that forgiveness is possible, a reverence reminiscent of Wordsworth's "Intimations of Immortality" ode, a gratitude for the many ways that love touches the world.

Arguably the most surprising day of all came when my husband asked me to pray the rosary in his presence. The joke was on me that afternoon, for (shame on me) I'd never said a formal rosary and had to excuse myself to go find the text. I didn't need that crib sheet for long, though, since Ford not only kept asking, but appeared so calmed and reassured by that venerable prayer that I took to reciting it as he slept.

The capstone of our brief, unarticulated, but beautiful mutual faith-life came seven days before his death, when I celebrated a homemade Easter Vigil. "You used to love it," he upbraided me. "How can you not go this year?" But it was unthinkable to leave

him for three hours at that point when his health was so precipitously declining, so I resorted to a domestic approximation.
I planned to light an unofficial Easter candle in the living room
rather than the bedroom (for I feared the lengthy expression of
faith might be too much for him, and, frankly, I was shy), sing
the *Exsultet* and the responsorial psalms, read aloud the Scriptures
and prayers, and consume the host our Newman Center director,
a kind nun, had provided to me when I confessed my intention
("You've been a Eucharistic minister, so you can minister to the
homebound, and this year, that's you!" she'd proclaimed with such
conviction that I couldn't refuse, though the logic seemed iffy).
That would have to be good enough, this year.

As the daylight waned on Easter Eve, Ford rested quietly in bed,
half dozing, half watching the light change on a distant mountain ridge. When the room grew almost dark and I put down my
knitting and rose to go begin the "service," my husband turned,
reaching insistently for my arm. "No," he said. "In here. I want to
hear it. Please."

Thus that year my Easter candle stood on the broad wooden
sill of our bedroom window, and I sight-sang the *Exsultet* leaning
against a reading pillow on the bed beside my husband. "Rejoice,
heavenly powers! Sing choirs of angels!" As I requested that our
candle in the window "mingle with the lights of heaven," I saw
the first stars glowing behind it, a blessing I'll always remember.
"Beautiful," Ford whispered.

Beginning with Genesis, I worked my way through the mornings and evenings of creation, through Moses, Abraham, and Isaac.
As I voiced Ezekiel's proclamation of mercy—"For I will take you
away from among the nations . . . and bring you back to your
own land. . . . I will give you a new heart and place a new spirit
within you . . . you shall be my people, and I will be your God"
(36:24-28)—Ford's hand again gently touched my arm.

With the last quiet notes of "Ye Sons and Daughters" (a recessional in a minor key had seemed right), I extinguished the candle
and eased my warmth under the covers next to my husband's frail

body. His breath flowed deeply and rhythmically, and I heard none of the anxious stirring or panicked murmuring that so often characterized those days. Allowing its cadence to draw me down with him, I slept as I'd not slept for a long time before, nor would for a long time again.

I don't mean to pose this story as a literal conversion testimony, please understand. Ford never proclaimed Jesus to be his personal Lord and Savior, nor attended confession or a real Catholic Mass (though a priest he'd met and liked did come to bless him on the final day). Yet after he passed, it seemed beyond inappropriate to fear for his immortal soul . . . although my own, as I've suggested, felt for some time in real jeopardy.

✦ ✦ ✦

"What do you think happens when we die?" a friend who is unchurched but God-curious asked me recently. I said what seems obvious: we can't know because heaven is a realm beyond our possible ken; the depictions we do have are metaphors framed from our limited intelligence but probably onto something at least symbolically; whatever it is, it's going to be good, somehow bringing our spirits into the presence of the loving Mystery who created us for a dignified, meaningful, unique life and has tenderly labored all along to encourage us to become who we were created to be.

I have, however, stood on the threshold of that "whatever it is" several times as I lay the quiet, comforting hands of hospice massage on people in the process of dying—experiences which have suggested what it might be like to be a faithful soul in transition. Though painkillers mercifully calm those under doctors' care in this day and age, I believe that I've seen a pattern of easier passage for those who understand themselves as giving in—or giving over—to God. In such cases a sense of the ineffable suffuses the room—a mystery, a calmness that feels sacred, that calms and reassures the watchers, too. That was true, also, at the hour of my husband's death.

What I believe we *can* be sure about is that the Shepherd of our souls wants us to come home. Whether we've been in the habit of retreating into skepticism, or balking at divine summons or attempting to escape them, or wincing away in fear or talking back, or bowing our heads in compliant reverence when God calls, God is by nature infinitely persistent, infinitely tenacious, infinitely creative in shaping the evolving circumstances of our lives to foster our love and faith, even unto death. Perhaps even *after* death, if you believe my friend Origen.

All we can do, in the meantime, is to live our lives as faithfully as we can, trusting with all the equanimity and good humor we can muster that God's mercy will not fail us, and that all this vexed and holy business of being human ultimately will end well.

Holy Mary, Mother of God and our human sister, pray for us. Guide us and inspire us by your example to face with courage the angels of calling who burst upon us without warning, without wanting. Help us to accept that learning to say "yes" does not diminish us, but opens the way to new life.

Fra Filippo Lippi, *The Annunciation*, 1443.

Afterword

One of my favorite elderly hospice clients recently lost her husband, her sweetheart since adolescence. When I visited a few days after his funeral Mass, Catalina was a changed person from her usual lively self. Her dementia, previously come-and-go, had engulfed her, and she slumped in her recliner in what looked like a stupor of weakness. Though she did recognize and greet me, she lapsed quickly again into semi-consciousness, periodically weeping, and tears filled my eyes, too, as I tried to comfort her with gentle touch, praying for the higher love I sometimes feel to flow through my hands.

"We're afraid she's decided just to go with him," her son lamented. "They were such lovebirds that it's hard to imagine them without each other, and I think she feels that way, too."

If anybody could set her mind to going, it's probably Catalina. Though tiny and frail, all who love her know her to be a determined woman, one who regularly worked multiple jobs to supplement her husband's income as they raised their six children, tireless in tending a big garden and fruit trees, canning, cooking; an excellent seamstress who made their children's clothes (and extra cash by sewing costumes for the university's theater department); a beloved (and very interactive) "abuelita" for hosts of grandchildren and great-grandchildren; a constant companion and support for her husband in old age. Now, though, the spark had vanished.

Back at home that evening, I couldn't help but remember how fervently I had wanted to be "beamed up" quickly after Ford died in 2002, how energetically I'd supplicated the heavens for that "blessing." It felt to me that evening as if Catalina might just be successful in effectuating what had been my own heart's desire, as some elderly couples seem to do when they pass within days or weeks of each other. Catalina was refusing food, and her heart-rate and breathing were extremely unhealthy; but something less medically objective, something strongly intentional, seemed at the root of her debility.

To my surprise I felt a rush of envy sweep through me—bone-deep, instinctive. Had Catalina found that secret I hadn't been able to discover, twenty years ago? What was wrong with me, that I hadn't figured it out?

But, I told myself, if it did transpire that Catalina possessed that secret and could teach it to me, of course I'd have to finish this book first, and the next one, too. I'd want to wait until Shelley, my former student-turned-daughter, retires (still five years, darn it) so we can travel together as we've been longing to do. I've promised my goddaughter that we'll go back to Norway before long, this time to the far north since we didn't get to see it the first time. I'm eager to deepen my friendship with Bridget, to spend more time with Anna. I want to knit for various little ones of my acquaintance as they grow, help my naughty but darling grey kitten learn her manners, and watch over my older two kitties as they age. There's a lot more communing with the Caribou National Forest to do, and turning seasons to watch from my window, and music to explore, and books to read, and old friendships to cultivate. And I can't leave my current hospice patients in the lurch, and Heritage Health Services keeps giving me new ones all the time.

Abruptly I was shaking my head, mock lamenting and rejoicing all at once, smiling as I believe Alessandro Allori's Mary does at the rush of incoming revelation.

I've been had, in the holiest and most loving of ways.

✦ ✦ ✦

While planning this book, I assumed that for symmetry's sake this afterword would be illustrated by a painting depicting one of those regal Renaissance Marys who'd made me feel so inadequate in 2004. Standing tall and wrapped in a confidence that appeared to proclaim: "Of course it's me!"—even condescending to Gabriel—they seemed to possess a certainty of being loved and approved of by God that utterly escaped me back then. I imagined that as this book came to its close, I'd be suggesting that such spiritual confidence is potentially available to all of us, that if we learn how to get comfortable with co-creative surrender, we will be able to stand tall and serene in the presence of a loving God, taking justified pride in our active participation in the unfolding of divine will.

But a funny thing happened last week when I went looking for the perfect image to focus this afterword's meditation: I couldn't find *any* Marys as absolutely queenly as I'd remembered, any Virgins so absolutely triumphant, so unruffled in their confidence that a viewer could remotely imagine them as "smug," as I'd once judged the images I remembered from Florence.

Trying to see what I'd once seen, I lingered for a long time over a painting I remembered singling out back in 2004 as an exemplar of preternatural compliance, Fra Filippo Lippi's 1443 Annunciation, painted for the nuns of the Suore Murate Convent in Florence. And indeed, twenty years along, I could see why I might once have thought of this Mary as dauntingly regal. She stands in what one art critic has termed a "sumptuous Renaissance palace," a space regally constructed with elegant arches and lavish decoration. She's beautifully dressed, with a golden halo like a crown on her head. As might be expected of a queen or noblewoman, she's the largest figure in the painting, framed dramatically in one of those arches. This Virgin Mary is taking Gabriel's news with composure, standing very upright rather than kneeling. It's Gabriel himself who's vulnerable in this version of Luke's story, overwhelmed by Mary's presence, kneeling meekly before her, not daring to make eye contact, staring down as if stunned.

As I returned after two decades to this image, however, I saw the signs that softened that original interpretation of "perfect confidence." This Mary's head is bowed like so many others', indicating submission. Her expression is thoughtful rather than triumphant, as if, like Remi's Madonna, she's going inward to ponder complex, even worrisome matters. She puts her right hand to her heart, something people do when they've gotten a shock and need to center and quiet themselves—a gesture Fra Angelico's Mary might have made. She's a mixture of contradictions, in other words—regal, yes, but also humble, confident, and submissive—hardly the condescending, perfectly assorted queen I once perceived. She's a faithful human woman, in other words, someone who, like all the rest of us, will sometimes quake and inwardly struggle, even while loving God absolutely, even as she dedicates herself to following the divine will.

How could I not have noticed these qualifying details before? And what was I going to use to illustrate the triumphant theme I'd anticipated for this afterword?

The truth about where all those unapproachably queenly Marys might possibly have gone—which I'm betting you might have already guessed—dawned quickly enough. What had changed was *me*. Possessed by guilt at the time I first encountered these paintings, I'd unconsciously interpreted them as judgmental commentaries on my own flailing, anger, and resistance. Rather than expecting mercy and understanding from the Mother of God as she was pictured by these painters, I'd assumed that such a one could hardly understand—much less be willing to companion—a wretch like me.

Back in 2004 it had taken the much more obvious signs of discomfort in Fra Angelico's Mary to help me imagine that the Mother of God might just understand what I was going through. Even at that, the me who sat on the steps staring at that fresco still had so much to learn about God's patience and tolerance. How self-absorbed my old self seems to me now, with her exceptionalist *there is no sorrow like my sorrow* wailing, her assumption of being uniquely singled out for punishment, her naive assumption that others found it easy to bow in acquiescence before circumstances they never wished for themselves. How poorly I then understood Mary, and myself.

Today I can only marvel at how richly I've been blessed in the two decades since that afternoon in 2004—blessed by divine patience, blessed by that series of "pesterings" that have filled those years with good work, happy self-discovery, a more grown-up understanding of faith and relationship with the divine, even a measure of peace beyond what I could have imagined I'd ever feel again on that bleak November day.

Had I been given a choice in the prime of life, would I have chosen the way I'm living now instead of old age in a ripely joyful marriage with my beloved? Of course not. But if this is the way things had to be, it's been a very interesting alternative, and a good one.

"Yes," it seems, comes in many forms and assumes many tones . . . and adapts to many timetables.

May God's patient love support you, too, whenever and however you're challenged to gather your courage, trust in grace, and say "yes."

Pocatello, Idaho
October 30, 2023

Appendix

Luke's Account of the Annunciation and Magnificat

The Annunciation, Luke 1:26-38

In the sixth month, the angel Gabriel was sent from God to a town of Galilee called Nazareth, to a virgin betrothed to a man named Joseph, of the house of David, and the virgin's name was Mary. And coming to her, he said, "Hail, favored one! The Lord is with you." But she was greatly troubled at what was said and pondered what sort of greeting this might be. Then the angel said to her, "Do not be afraid, Mary, for you have found favor with God. Behold, you will conceive in your womb and bear a son, and you shall name him Jesus. He will be great and will be called Son of the Most High, and the Lord God will give him the throne of David his father, and he will rule over the house of Jacob forever, and of his kingdom there will be no end. But Mary said to the angel, "How can this be, since I have no relations with a man?" And the angel said to her in reply, "The holy Spirit will come upon you, and the power of the Most High will overshadow you. Therefore the child to be born will be called holy, the Son of God. And behold, Elizabeth, your relative, has also conceived a son in her old age, and this is the sixth month for her who was called barren; for nothing will be impossible for God." Mary said,

"Behold, I am the handmaid of the Lord. May it be done to me according to your word." Then the angel departed from her.

Mary's *Magnificat*, Luke 1:46-55

And Mary said:
"My soul proclaims the greatness of the Lord;
my spirit rejoices in God my savior.
For he has looked upon his handmaid's lowliness;
behold, from now on will all ages call me blessed.
The Mighty One has done great things for me,
and holy is his name.
His mercy is from age to age
to those who fear him.
He has shown might with his arm,
dispersed the arrogant of mind and heart.
He has thrown down the rulers from their thrones
but lifted up the lowly.
The hungry he has filled with good things;
the rich he has sent away empty.
He has helped Israel his servant,
remembering his mercy,
according to his promise to our fathers,
to Abraham and to his descendants forever."

Notes

Introduction

1. Fr. Jean-Pierre de Caussade, *Abandonment to Divine Providence*, trans. E. J. Strickland, ed. J. Ramiére (Gastonia, NC: Tan Classics, 2010).

2. In an extreme example of this "Whatever, God!" theology of human passivity, a writer in the network bloggersforthekingdom proclaims, "Surrendering to God is literally giving up. . . . It is telling God that we are not big enough to deal with our worries, and He must take over."

3. Tolkien expresses this idea in "On Fairy Stories," originally presented as a talk at the University of St. Andrews in 1939, collected in *The Tolkien Reader* (New York: Del Rey, 1986).

4. You might begin with St. Thomas Aquinas's *Summa Theologica*, or St. Augustine's *Confessions*, for example.

5. Henri Nouwen, *Henri Nouwen on Suffering and Joy* (Rockville, MD: Now You Know Media, 2017).

6. For an accessible overview of such research along with consideration of how aesthetic elements of art contribute to viewer response, see Ladislav Kesner and Jiri Horáček's article, "Empathy-Related Responses to Depicted People in Art Works," *Frontiers in Psychology* 8 (2017): 228.

7. See, for example, Zane Wilkinson et al., "The Influence of Empathy on the Perceptual Response to Visual Arts," *Psychology of Aesthetics, Creativity, and the Arts* (2021).

8. I've chosen Renaissance paintings not only because they're beautiful works of art that might already be familiar to you (and because the annunciation was an extremely popular subject during those centuries, thus affording many possible examples) but also to establish some consistencies: (1) all are painted in a representational style which, while somewhat varied during the years chosen for this book, has similar enough conventions that fair comparison-contrast based on treatment of subject matter is possible; and (2) all the artists here represented

shared the same consistent articles of Catholic faith regarding Mary and the event itself, and thus variation can be seen as individual expression.

9. John M. Carvalho, "Annunciations: Figuring the Feminine in Renaissance Art," *Contemporary Aesthetics (Journal Archive)* 13 (2015), https://digitalcommons.risd.edu/liberalarts_contempaesthetics/vol13/iss1/10/. Fra Roberto Caracciolo of Lecce, who identified these stages in a 1494 sermon on the annunciation, described them as *conturbatio* (disquiet), *cogitatio* (reflection), *interrogatio* (inquiry), *humiliatio* (submission), and *meritatio* (response or "merit").

10. Henri Nouwen, *The Return of the Prodigal Son: A Story of Homecoming* (New York: Doubleday, 1992).

Chapter One

1. *Gaudete et exsultate*, 2018; Message for World Day for Vocations, 2018; Message for World Day for Vocations, 2023.

2. Joseph Bolin's *Paths of Love: The Discernment of Vocation According to the Teaching of Aquinas, Ignatius, and Pope John Paul II* (CreateSpace Independent Publishing Platform, 2008) offers a good sampler of how great writers and thinkers of the church have approached the topic.

3. For evocative illustrations of this phenomenon, take a look at the memoirs of men and women called at a very young age to religious vocation, which so often chronicle "honeymoon" periods when they dreamed idealistically of extraordinary service and never-failing communion with the divine. See, for example St. Thérèse of Lisieux's *The Story of a Soul*.

4. Biographical details and quotations from contemporaries about Pontormo's life are taken from Giorgio Vasari's *The Lives of the Artists* (1550/1568, originally titled *The Lives of the Most Excellent Painters, Sculptors, and Architects*), trans. Julia Conway Bondanella and Peter Bondanella (Oxford: Oxford University Press, 2008).

5. For the details of St. Francis de Sales' thoughts on vocation, see his books *Introduction to the Devout Life* (originally published in 1609), and *Finding God's Will for You* (Manchester, NH: Sophia Institute Press, 1998).

6. And I, for one, have been long haunted by the sense that if I'd been Mary, the guilt that my pregnancy had inadvertently caused the death of so many other children while mine survived would have been overwhelming, even given the awareness that my son was destined to go about God's essential business.

7. "Servant Song" by Donna Marie McGargill, OSM, © 1984, OCP. All rights reserved. Used with permission.

Chapter Two

1. Guilio Carlo Argan, *Storia dell'arte italiana*, 3rd ed. (Florence: Sansoni, 2002), 153; Fabbio Indìo Massimo Poppi and Peter Kravanja, "Annuntiatio Domini: Metaphoric Conceptualization and Gesture Analysis in Painted Representations of the Annunciation," *Public Journal of Semiotics* 8 (2017): 26–45.

2. For the town in which it was originally hung.

3. More recent depictions of the scene show her looking stricken to the point of breakdown, as in Dante Gabriel Rossetti's 1850 painting, and the Irish artist Adam Pomeroy's twentieth-century interpretation. If you're interested, an internet post ("A Potpourri of Contemporary Annunciation Art") of March 25, 2019 (https://tmblr.co/ZVz2Ix2h5dhY1), includes Pomeroy's work along with many others which depict the scene in widely varied, very evocative, potentially controversial ways. To get a sense of the breadth of ways the scene has been depicted, you might search out one of the several pictorial anthologies of Annunciation art; among my favorites (including works between 1432 and 1984) is *Annunciation*, ed. Julia Hasting (London: Phaidon, 2000). For a deeper dive into analysis of such art, Sarah Drummond's *Divine Conception: The Art of the Annunciation* (London: Unicorn, 2018) is a very good place to begin.

4. As Sally Read writes, for example, in *Annunciation: A Call to Faith in a Broken World* (San Francisco: Ignatius Press, 2019), 21.

5. See Elizabeth Lev's *How Catholic Art Saved the Faith: The Triumph of Beauty and Truth in Counter-Reformation Art* (Manchester, NH: Sophia Institute Press, 2018) for a detailed discussion of this fascinating subject.

6. William Hood, *Fra Angelico at San Marco* (London: BCA [by arrangement with Yale University Press], 1993), 21.

7. The term is my own, first voiced as I grappled to explain how I was feeling to a very patient psychologist.

8. Especially helpful articles about sensemaking include Jeff Grabmeier, "This Is Your Brain Detecting Patterns," *Science Daily*, May 31, 2018, Ohio State University, https://www.sciencedaily.com/releases/2018/05/180531114642.htm; and Richard J. Cordes, "Making Sense of Sensemaking: What It Is and What It Means for Pandemic Research," August 27, 2020, https://www.atlanticcouncil .org/blogs/geotech-cues/making-sense-of-sensemaking-what-it-is-and-what-it -means-for-pandemic-research/. For more technical, fascinating detail about the social adaptation inherent in sensemaking, see B. Duchaine et al., "Evolutionary Psychology and the Brain," which argues that "the human brain is a set of computational machines, each of which was designed by natural selection to solve adaptive problems faced by our hunter-gatherer ancestors" (225); *Current Opinion in Neurobiology* 11 (April 2001): 225–30.

9. Beth Hewett, *Grief on the Road to Emmaus: A Monastic Approach to Journeying with the Bereaved* (Collegeville, MN: Liturgical Press, 2023).

10. It's telling, I believe, that the subject of the treatise in which these remarks appear was the book of Job, that story of a good man seemingly besieged by God (or, at least, besieged with God's permission)—a seminal work for those in liminal space, as I suggest below (*Moralia, sive Exposition in Job* [*Morals, or Narrative on Job*, vol. 1, par. 1; 570–95 AD]). For another saintly example of striking resistance—one echoing Lotto's painting—see the story of St. John Vianney, who literally ran away from his parish in Ars several times, seeking to escape the consequences of extraordinary, exhausting popularity as a confessor (as recounted in Margaret Trouncer, *Saint Jean-Marie Vianney: Curé of Ars* [New York: Sheed and Ward, 1959]).

11. Elizabeth Johnson, *Truly Our Sister: A Theology of Mary in the Communion of Saints* (New York: Continuum, 2003), 248–49.

12. A great deal of scholarly work considers the story's archetypal, larger-than-life quality. Its details have been determined to be ahistorical, and versions of it appear in the sacred texts of other faiths, including Jewish literature and the Quran. Its tone has even been debated; some scholars, for example, argue that it might have been constructed as a satire of Jewish beliefs. See, for example, J. Harold Ellens, ed., *Psychological Hermeneutics for Biblical Themes and Texts: A Festschrift in Honor of Wayne G. Rollins*, T&T Clark Biblical Studies (London: T&T Clark, 2012); and Ehud Ben Zvi, *The Signs of Jonah: Reading and Rereading in Ancient Yehud*, Journal for the Study of the Old Testament Supplement Series 367 (Sheffield: Sheffield Academic Press, 2003).

13. John J. Boucher, "Grappling with Guilt: The Gift of God's GPS," October 29, 2020, https://www.catholicdigest.com/amp/faith/grappling-with-guilt/.

14. Another reference to Joni Mitchell's "Court and Spark." The phrase "my kind words find their way back to me" is lifted from another song from that era by the singer-songwriter Jackson Browne, "My Opening Farewell."

15. The phrase is Cyril Vollert's, from his book *A Theology of Mary*, St. Mary's Theology Series 3 (New York: Herder and Herder, 1965). And it's worth noting in the context of this book that painters have not been the only artists to associate the angst of uncertainty with Mary's annunciation: the seventeenth-century composer Heinrich Biber set the annunciation movement of his rosary-based *Mystery Sonatas* in the key of D-minor, a key in his time understood as denoting anxiety and fearfulness of soul. See Christian Schubart's 1784 essay "A History of Key Characteristics in the 18th and Early 19th Centuries," discussed in Kat Wilson's article "The Heartbreak Key," August 18, 2021, *Rolling Stone*, https://www.rollingstone.com/pro/features/music-d-minor-saddest-key-121059.

Chapter Three

1. Reni's troubled life and artistic career are described in detail in Richard E. Spear's *The "Divine" Guido: Religion, Sex, Money and Art in the World of Guido Reni* (New Haven: Yale University Press, 1997). Marie de Medici's commission of this painting is mentioned in an article at https://themedicifamily.com/marie-de-medici, and the Wikipedia entry about Marie chronicles her political conniving.

2. For more detail, see https://www.hinduamerican.org/blog/what-are-the-four-stages-of-hindu-life/.

3. Richard Rohr, *Falling Upward: A Spirituality for the Two Halves of Life* (San Francisco: Jossey-Bass, 2011).

4. Gerard W. Hughes, *God of Surprises*, rev. ed. (London: Darton, Longman, and Todd, 2008), 11. The term "God of surprises" comes from the great twentieth-century theologian Karl Rahner.

5. Thomas Merton, *New Seeds of Contemplation* (1961; rpt. New York: New Directions, 2007).

6. That L'Arche provided Nouwen with the new freedom essential for spiritual growth is particularly evident in *The Return of the Prodigal Son: A Story of Homecoming* (New York: Doubleday, 1992), the book which inspired this book's use of art as a focus for meditation.

7. Many of Nouwen's books speak about discernment as a general practice and describe his personal experience of it. For a valuable overview, see the compilation of his writings, *Discernment: Reading the Signs of Daily Life*, with Michael J. Christensen and Rebecca J. Laird (New York: HarperOne, 2013). All quotes from Nouwen in this section are drawn from that volume.

8. Paragraph 2715 of the *Catechism* uses this phrase, said to have been conveyed to St. John Vianney by a pious peasant to describe his practice of contemplation. It's also repeated in James Martin, *Learning to Pray: A Guide for Everyone* (New York: HarperOne, 2021).

9. Nouwen himself, in fact, repeatedly found it difficult to focus when he undertook extended retreats, lapsing into despair, a feeling of invisibility, and aridity. See Michael Ford's *Wounded Prophet: A Portrait of Henri J.M. Nouwen* (New York: Doubleday, 1999), and Wil Hernandez, *Henri Nouwen: A Spirituality of Imperfection* (New York: Paulist, 2006).

10. *Butler's Lives of the Saints, Complete Edition*, edited, revised, and supplemented by Herbert J. Thurston, SJ, and Donald Attwater (Allen, TX: Christian Classics, 1956; rpt. 1996).

11. A sisterhood that includes the widow-saint who soon became my patron, the American educational pioneer St. Elizabeth Ann Seton.

Chapter Four

1. Allori had been appointed by his Medici patrons to a lucrative supplemental employment as director of a textile division in their enterprises, even as he was painting, and several other of his images—including Annunciations—also use fiber-arts details. And he's far from the only Renaissance artist to have fancied Mary as a practitioner of the fiber arts; indeed, images of her knitting, in particular (whether at the annunciation or in scenes of subsequent family life with the baby Jesus), are common enough that such figures have gained recognition as a minor subgenre known as "Knitting Madonnas." For a well-known and especially charming example, see Master Bertram's Buxtehude Altar (c. 1400–1410). An internet search for "Knitting Madonnas" will direct you to numerous short posts. See also the introduction to my book *Knitting as a Spiritual Path: Exploring a Wiser, Kinder, More Meaningful Life, One Stitch at a Time* (Chicago: ACTA, 2022).

2. https://www.finestresullarte.info/operadelgiorno/2014/322-alessandro-allori-annunciazione.php. This attribution is based on the circumstances of the painting's donation to the Accademia many years later.

3. For an overview of thinking about how humor works, see "Philosophy of Humor," in *The Stanford Encyclopedia of Humor* (2012, rev. ed. 2020), https://plato.stanford.edu/entries/humor.

4. James Martin, *Between Heaven and Mirth: Why Joy, Humor, and Laughter Are at the Heart of the Spiritual Life* (New York: HarperCollins, 2011), 88–92, 194–206.

5. Joan Chittister, *The Gift of Years: Growing Older Gracefully* (New York: Bluebridge, 2008).

6. Cited by the Population Research Bureau. See Paola Scommegna, "Happily Ever After? Research Offers Clues on What Shapes Happiness and Life after Age 65," April 6, 2023, https://www.prb.org/resources/happily-ever-after-research-offers-clues-on-what-shapes-happiness-and-life-satisfaction-after-age-65/.

7. Pope Francis established the World Day for Grandparents and the Elderly in 2021, and his addresses on that occasion (celebrated on the fourth Sunday in July) sound such themes. See in particular the address he delivered in 2023, which proclaimed, "Let us honor them, neither depriving ourselves of their company nor depriving them of ours. May we never allow the elderly to be cast aside!" (https://www.vaticannews.va/en/pope/news/2023-06/pope-message-for-world-day-of-grandparents-and-elderly-2023.html).

8. Edward Mote, "My Hope Is Built on Nothing Less" (1834).

9. For an example of such work, see Taylor Ross's June 4, 2019, article published under the auspices of the University of Notre Dame, "The Severity of

Universal Salvation," https://churchlifejournal.nd.edu/articles/the-severity-of
-universal-salvation/. Morwenna Ludlow's *Universal Salvation: Eschatology in
the Thought of Gregory of Nyssa and Karl Rahner* (Oxford: Clarendon Press, 2000)
traces this theme more broadly. Joseph W. Trigg's *Origen*, The Early Church
Fathers (London: Routledge, 1998), discusses both the theologian's life and
his writing.

For Further Reading

Chittister, Joan. *The Gift of Years: Growing Older Gracefully.* New York: Bluebridge, 2008.

De Caussade, Jean-Pierre. *Abandonment to Divine Providence.* Translated by E. J. Srickland, edited by J. Ramiére. Gastonia, NC: Tan Classics, 2010.

Drummond, Sarah. *Divine Conception: The Art of the Annunciation.* London: Unicorn, 2018.

Hasting, Julia, ed. *Annunciation.* London: Phaidon, 2000.

Hewett, Beth. *Grief on the Road to Emmaus: A Monastic Approach to Journeying with the Bereaved.* Collegeville, MN: Liturgical Press, 2023.

Hughes, Gerard W. *God of Surprises.* Rev. ed. London: Darton, Longman, and Todd, 2008.

Johnson, Elizabeth A. *Truly Our Sister: A Theology of Mary in the Communion of the Saints.* New York: Continuum, 2003.

Martin, James. *Between Heaven and Mirth: Why Joy, Humor, and Laughter Are at the Heart of the Spiritual Life.* New York: HarperCollins, 2011.

Martin, James. *Learning to Pray: A Guide for Everyone.* New York: HarperOne, 2021.

Merton, Thomas. *New Seeds of Contemplation.* 1961; reprinted New York: New Directions, 2007.

Nouwen, Henri. *Discernment: Reading the Signs of Daily Life.* With Michael J. Christensen and Rebecca J. Laird. New York: HarperOne, 2013.

Nouwen, Henri. *The Return of the Prodigal Son: A Story of Homecoming.* New York: Doubleday, 1992.

Rohr, Richard. *Falling Upwards: A Spirituality for the Two Halves of Life.* San Francisco: Jossey-Bass, 2011.

Swetnam, Susan. *In the Mystery's Shadow: Reflections on Caring for the Elderly and Dying.* Collegeville, MN: Liturgical Press, 2019.